(RE)BOOT YOUR CAREER

A BLUEPRINT FOR FINDING YOUR CALLING, MARKETING YOURSELF, AND LANDING GREAT GIGS

TIM RAGAN AND PAUL GIBBONS

Dedication

While data show that many people are unhappy in their jobs or unfulfilled by their careers, few decide to do something about that. Fewer act. Fewer still persevere in reaching their full potential.

This book is for those who persevere.

Text by Tim Ragan and Paul Gibbons

Tim Ragan: http://careerconstructors.com

Paul Gibbons: http://paulgibbons.net

First edition – September 2016

ISBN 10 – 1537710699

ISBN 13 – 9781537710693

TABLE OF CONTENTS

Preface:
About This Book

Why Should I Read This Book?

We find, in our work as consultants and coaches, that people struggle with seven categories of career problems. If one or more of these sound like you, then *(Re)boot Your Career* will help you get the results you want.

1. **"I'm just starting off, and don't have a clue what I want to do with** my **life."** You're the reason we called this book (Re)boot and not Reboot, because you are looking to boot up your career for the first time. Our blueprint will provide you with self-awareness and tools to do that. The sooner you start a process such as this, the greater the lifetime benefits.

2. **"I've applied for countless roles, but haven't landed a job."** We often hear about people who apply for dozens (or hundreds) of roles online and don't receive any feedback, let alone an interview. If this is you, you need to do two things: (a) rebrand your application materials, but more importantly b) circumvent the "numbers game" that is online job applications. We provide you with some useful tools to accomplish this.

3. **"My current job is unfulfilling."** Perhaps you are unchallenged, coasting through the day, feeling as if you use 10% of your skills and abilities. You don't necessarily want to leave your organization; however, you definitely need to figure out how to enjoy your work more, find opportunities to do more meaningful work, and reap the rewards of your greater contribution. Our insights on finding your passion and developing a personal brand can help you find more fulfilling work in your current company.

4. **"I'm not sure I'm in the right line of work."** Perhaps you are second-guessing your decision to work in a certain field. You have invested much in your education, and aren't sure how to transfer your education and skills to another environment. We show you how to articulate your capabilities and package them as highly transferable.

5. **"I'm in a career transition."** You have decided to leave your company, or perhaps the organization laid you off. You might be trying to reenter the workforce after having raised a family or finished school. You might want to work in another industry, or just want to shift gears, learn new skills, and set out on a new path. You need to navigate through the uncertainty of a major

career transition and discover your perfect job. Follow our process for a successful transition.

6. **"I'm soloing."** You left the traditional employee role to embark on your own. You might refer to yourself as an independent, a freelancer, a consultant, a contractor, or a "solopreneur." You want your soloing to be based on a realistic assessment of your skills and values. We will help you develop a solid value proposition and guide you through communicating that message to your target audience.

7. **"I'm of retirement age, but have no desire to retire."** While you have formally retired from your job, days filled with golf, cable news, and shopping aren't fulfilling. You know you have more to give back, but aren't sure what that looks like. The possibilities seem almost endless. This book will put structure and discipline into how to make that transition.

Other clients have had different situations, but these seven are the most common. Many people live with these circumstances for decades, either from not having the courage to change or a road map of how to do so.

How Exactly Will *(Re)boot Your Career* Help Me?

This book provides a blueprint, tools, and action steps to make better choices and create magnificent opportunities.

The four sections of this book are building blocks that help you develop clarity, sense of purpose, and disciplined habits to help you advance your career. Some of the tools, such as the résumé and social media tools, can be used on a standalone basis. Despite this, we recommend that you take on the book sequentially, because it provides a holistic process that will lend power to your résumé and social media presence. This, we think, produces greater results.

By reading this book and completing the numerous exercises, you will:

Understand yourself better and your career choices;

Grow confident in your career niche and the contribution you can make to your communities and society;

Learn to **express your passion**, and how your uniqueness adds value;

Understand how to **communicate your uniqueness** to help you find meaningful opportunities;

Learn how to **create a brand** and **build networks** that deliver opportunity.

In short, you will become more confident and proficient in your communications: your dialogue, writing and conversation skills, use of social media, and networking abilities. You will be well on your way to developing **career mastery**.

(Re)boot Your Career breaks down those steps into four sections:

Introduction — The Big Picture—Better understand today's workplaces and job markets and how those affect your career

Section I — The Inside Job—Discover more about who you are and what you care about (your personality and values and how those affect your career decisions)

Section 2 — Developing a Personal Brand—Construct the story that maximizes the impression you make (your personal brand and social media profile)

Section 3 — The Outside Job – Modern Job-Hunting Skills—Acquire new job-hunting skills (networking, using social media, attending information meetings, interviewing)

Sections 1, 2, and 3 are further broken into "stages" and "steps." In each section, we present a number of concepts, or **stages**, that are critical to understand. Each stage then contains a number of specific **steps** that you will complete as you work through this book.

How is (Re)boot Your Career Different from Other Books?

There are dozens of other great career books. Although rich in insights, none that we know of provides a blueprint for how to go from asking,

"What do I want to do with my life?" to stating, "This role is perfect for me!" to using the right tools to help realize that dream.

We help you answer that question, translate the answer into practical roles, communicate your passion and abilities, and navigate the complexities of the 21st century job market.

How Do I Get Most Value from *(Re)boot Your Career*?

To get value from this book, you need to **take action**. It takes time to take action, and as every compulsive book buyer knows, books can pile up waiting to be read; don't do this to your career. We recommend a five-stage process for getting the most from this book.

1. First, quickly scan through the book from beginning to end to develop a clear sense of how the material builds on itself and how the work assignments help you build your complete story and supporting tool kit. This scan shouldn't take more than one hour.

2. Second, after scanning the book and understanding the flow, set up a minimum of one designated hour a week (for example, Sunday evenings, or Monday mornings). During these periods, read through the book more deeply, reflect on the content, and work through the specific steps in order. You are sure to make steady progress on the exercises within, and that progress is itself highly motivational.

3. Third, friends can help. We recommend you tell them you are reading this book, perhaps inviting one or two of them to check in with you occasionally to see if you are making progress. Throughout the book, we identify different work exercises you will benefit from greatly by sharing them with your confidants.

4. Fourth, invest in a quality journal where you will take notes, complete exercises, and jot down insights. When we ask you to reflect on things, the insight may not come right away—it may come a day later, or at night, or in the shower. You want to begin the practice of capturing those reflections, jotting down bullets, mind-maps, or even just pictures.

5. Fifth, go to: www.careerconstructors.com/rebootyourcareer/ website, where you can sign up for free downloads of tools, insights, and tips to help you on your career journey.

Who Are We and Why Did We Write This Book?

We see and interact with many people who feel unfulfilled. There is a lot of untapped human potential all around us, and we think we would all be better off if somehow that potential could be unleashed. People would flourish; organizations would be less toxic, numerous positive outcomes and opportunities would exist. We can help by sharing our collective knowledge throughout this book.

Paul's story

Today I combine a passion for science and philosophy with nearly four decades of business experience. My books and public speaking help people apply research (psychology, philosophy, sociology, economics) in their lives as business leaders, particularly in leading change. You can find out more about those other books and find videos, articles, podcasts, and public talks at www.paulgibbons.net.

My career, however, got off to a rough start. Although I was book smart, finishing college at nineteen, I was not too smart when it came to career choices. In an act of teenage rebellion (and mostly because my parents thought so little of the profession), I turned to economics, then Wall Street, and by 27, had the expensive sports car, but was burned out and washed up. Despite this unhappy start, I am immensely grateful I realized so young that no amount of money can compensate for an unfulfilling career.

For the next five years, I tried one thing after another: getting a Ph.D. in neuroscience, pursuing careers in software sales and computer programming, running a bridge club, and starting a biotech company. I enjoyed none of those and kept bouncing. I finally landed a job with PricewaterhouseCoopers (PwC). Trading "skills" (mostly math and cursing loudly across the trading room) did not transfer well into a corporate environment, so PwC retrained me from the bottom up. I attended about 20 days of training a year, during which I also completed two masters' degrees.

These courses forced me to take a serious look at myself, and that self-investigation birthed the career that has lasted 25 years, first as a consultant, then as an entrepreneur. Each year, using some of the tools I found, developed, or refined, I review my career, what I've achieved (and not), and how my career goals for the year contribute to my life's mission. This makes me something of an expert in pivoting—making big career changes such as from full-time employment to entrepreneur, and from entrepreneur to author.

Part of my career today involves coaching people who find themselves with career dilemmas, or in an existential funk called "I hate what I'm doing, but I'm not sure I can do anything else, and I have a mortgage and two kids in college." I've counseled hundreds of people about the way out of such conundrums.

My passion for careers, and therefore for writing this book, stems from a) all those years of getting it wrong, b) having had great success using the tools we share with you today, and c) helping people shift direction in life-changing ways.

Tim's story

I am the owner/operator of Career Constructors, a coaching and performance consulting firm that helps individuals, work teams, and organizations thrive in change and find purpose and success in their endeavors. I have arrived here, after some 30 years, with deep personal knowledge of what it takes to navigate organizational upheaval, to redesign one's career, to deliver successful engagements, and to discover one's purpose.

I completed an undergraduate degree in electrical engineering at the University of Alberta in Edmonton, my hometown. My first full-time job was building a medical laser system at the university. That piqued my interest in high-technology endeavors, and so I packed up and drove across the country to Ottawa, Canada's 'Silicon Valley North.' I started working for a global telecoms organization, and spent the next two decades working at four different global corporations on three different continents while earning an MBA through part-time studies. As someone who loves learning new things and is always keen to take on new challenges, I served in numerous management and executive roles, from R&D and business unit management to channel sales, manufacturing, finance, quality, portfolio planning, and strategy.

Operating at the leading edge of technology and globalization, it was a volatile industry going through wild swings of rapid growth and severe shrinkage, and my own career opportunities rose and fell with the industry. I eventually served a stint as the CEO of a venture capital funded technology startup. Shortly after signing up, the industry went through the telecoms meltdown of 2001, and I spent a few years trying to keep our small boat afloat and pivoting the company more times than I can remember.

With those corporate experiences behind me, I decided to go "independent" and hung out my shingle as a management consultant, some 14 years ago. My journey as an independent—combined with the volatile industry experiences I survived through—has brought the whole notion—and business—of more effective career management into focus for me, and ultimately spawned this book with Paul. Life as an independent removes many of our daily excuses for performance issues: if I do not like the projects I am working on, I have only myself to ask as to why I agreed to them in the first place. If I do not think my clients value my time and expertise highly enough, I have only myself to ask as to what is not working with my positioning and value proposition. If my inbox is not full, I have only myself to ask as to what the problem is and what I need to do about it.

Life as an independent is clarifying, exhilarating, and challenging. It's allowed me to stretch myself and discover my purpose, and what I want to dedicate my work to: out of my 14-year journey comes the tools and techniques that fill the pages of this book.

How we 'met'

As of this writing, we have actually never met! In 21st century style, we connected on LinkedIn a few years ago, where we discovered a mutual interest in business strategy. For whatever reason, our particular connection "stuck," and we started trying to figure out a collaborative project we could work on together.

Paul was just finishing a book (The Science of Organizational Change) and Tim had just recently published his first book (Through the Detox Prism), so our first effort was agreeing to read each other's book and provide an Amazon recommendation. Then we decided to try a podcast series together, recording ten-minute interviews with gurus about leadership in the 21st century.

At the beginning of 2016, we decided to write this book. Tim was just in the process of kicking off a major rethink and repositioning of his business

(Career Constructors), and wanted to use the book to accelerate his own work on tightening his company's overall methodology. Paul wanted to add another title to his Reboot series; thus, the mutually attractive collaboration of (Re)boot Your Career was born.

We share our history to show you a real-life illustration of how to use social media effectively to build your network (Section 2) and how to be open and flexible when it comes to recognizing and working opportunities (Section 3). It is not an exaggeration to state that the very existence of this book is the outcome of us following these same practices.

INTRODUCTION:
CAREERS IN THE 21ST CENTURY

In this introduction, we look at 13 ways the workforce has changed, the 7 most harmful career myths, and the 8 most important aspects of the career mindset.

13 Ways the Workforce Has Changed in the 21st Century

If one plays tennis using the rules and tools of golf, the results are likely to be poor. The rules of work, employment, and career are vastly different from those of a quarter century ago, and "players" (people managing their careers) have to play by the new rules. We have included some general observations below, but the career-minded professional should also follow industry-/skill-specific trends. There are great resources available which predict the rise or fall of various occupations, or which are vulnerable to foreign competition or competition from developments in machine intelligence.

Here is our take on 13 global megatrends in the workforce:

1. **Globalization.** By some measures, and after a century at the top of the economic heap, the United States is now the world's second-largest economy, and by the middle of the century, it may be third. As globalization continues, the number of people assigned to work outside their home country will double within a decade.

Career message: Facility in working across cultures is no longer optional.

2. **Global talent.** The flip side of globalization is talent mobility. Workers in Western economies must compete not just with the best in their country for jobs, but the best from developing economies (particularly Asia). For example, China and India graduate between 500,000 and 1,000,000 engineers per year.

Career message: Global competition increases the necessity for getting your career and development right.

3. **Free agents.** Within a decade, half of workers will be soloing (as freelancers, contractors, solopreneurs, or "uberized"). This trend allows employers to manage fixed costs and respond to shifts in demand. At the same time, workers can make more flexible lifestyle choices and potentially earn more than in traditional employment.

Career message: Business development skills are no longer just for salespeople, and technological mastery (of collaboration tools) is no longer just for geeks.

4. **Project-based businesses**. The movie industry brings specialists together from several for projects. Once the project ends, the "business" disbands. In response to demands for greater agility, businesses are becoming project-based (or hybrids of project and traditional structures).

Career message: Project management is a core skill, not a specialist or an elective one.

5. **Remote working.** Even people with traditional 9 to 5 jobs will not be "suiting up and showing up." The office is no longer the center of production for most people, and managing virtual relationships is more important than ever. The idea of an office, or even a desk, may become an anachronism.

Career message: You will work with many people you will never meet or not know well. Managing virtual relationships across countries and time zones is essential.

6. **Always "on."** Whether it's an email on your phone or software that pings whenever your Delhi colleague uploads a presentation, interruptions never cease. Meetings happen across time zones at odd hours.

Career message: This means an increased need for self-management, knowing how to shut the virtual office door and disconnect. Those who cannot say no or manage the underlying interruptions and expectations will have extreme costs in their personal and professional lives.

7. **Retirement is retiring.** The idea that we educate ourselves until 22, work until 65, and then ride off into the sunset is now nonsense. As the average life span reaches into the 80s, more people are thinking about how to stay active and productive. Education becomes vital, as the skills required for success change every several years. More workers now think about career breaks and sabbaticals either for educational or personal reasons.

Career message: As you age, you need to continue to take the long view of your career, of where you want to go, and what skills you need to build.

8. **Aging.** We are getting older, not just individually (sniff), but collectively. The percentage of the world over 65 is the fastest growing demographic segment, and as we have suggested, fewer workers want to "go gentle into that good night."

Career message: Workers need the skills and maturity to work across generations, while older workers need to stay current. Organizations must completely rethink "up or out" cultures, where high-performers are promoted or move on when promotion is no longer likely.

9. **Data-driven, evidence-based.** The rise of analytics allows us to make decisions based on concrete data and scientifically proven models. This deluge of data, from sensors (Internet of Things), live videos, bioinformatics, and data mining will now drive decision-making across the business.

Career message: Using statistics, working with coders (data scientists), and using data visualization tools are becoming increasingly important.

10. **The rise of the machines.** During the early Industrial Revolution, workers threw their wooden shoes ("sabots") into machines to "sabotage" them, protesting the threat the machines posed to their jobs. No longer are machines just a threat to industrial jobs—many "knowledge-worker" jobs are now under siege from artificial intelligence.

Career message: Stay on top of these trends. They move much more slowly than media hype suggests; nevertheless, they move.

11. **Transparency.** All employers now check social media profiles, and our online behavior leaves a "digital exhaust" which is impossible to hide. However, such transparency cuts the other way also. Companies such as Glassdoor.com post employee reviews of company culture, rewards, engagement, and management prowess (or lack thereof).

Career message: You need to create a compelling online brand and actively manage possible negatives that employers might consider.

12. **Values matter.** One change in generational values is that younger workers care about their employer's footprint—the harm they do, or the good they could do, but don't. Thirty years ago, it would have been unusual to say, "I want to work someplace that is aligned with my values."

Career message: You need to be clear about your personal values, the values and practices you want your employer to have, and those you won't tolerate.

13. **Weak links and social media.** We're more connected now than ever through social media. We need to cultivate relationships through "weak links"—those LinkedIn and Twitter connections we know less well. Approximately 80% of jobs are found through networking, and those links connect us to the "employer ecosystems" and share inside knowledge and job referrals.

Career message: You need to build relationships with people on social media, particularly on LinkedIn. Most importantly, you need to follow a social media strategy that aligns with your own work styles, interests, and objectives.

These are the most important general trends for the workforce over the next few decades. The list can appear daunting, but you will only need to pay attention to the ones that affect your circumstances. For some, a general awareness of these trends is sufficient. Our main message is that you take heed of these and become a student of industry-specific trends in your field.

The 7 Most Harmful Career Myths

In our journey working with people in all professions, we have heard many myths that were either true once and now false, or were never true. These myths are destructive to career fulfillment. Which of these may be getting in your way?

1. **Myth: "It's the job."**

If you are unhappy at work, it may be the job, or more exactly, how your personality, skills or values fit the job, since some people presumably enjoy it. However, sometimes it is not the job, it is you. Some people lack the psychological equipment or skills to be happy (and there is a genetic component to happiness). Others may struggle forming positive working relationships. If you fall into one of these categories, you will bounce from job to job with the same lack of fulfillment. Nothing is more depressing than making the same mistake repeatedly, changing jobs because you are unhappy, then finding yourself just as unhappy. If you might fall into one of these categories, consider counseling—it can make a huge difference in your life.

2. **Myth: "I've come this far..."**

In psychology, this is called the "sunk-cost fallacy," and it keeps people in bad jobs, relationships, and investments for longer than necessary. If you are a specialist in the final years of your career, your ability to "pivot" your career will be limited, but in your 30s, this notion is faintly ridiculous. As Nietzsche said, "Many are stubborn in pursuit of the path they have chosen, few in pursuit of the goal." You want to be stubborn with regard to the goal, but flexible with regard to the path.

3. **Myth: "Your path in life will suddenly reveal itself to you in a flash of insight."**

Perhaps, but probably not. Most people learn what they like and dislike through trial and error, changing course along the way. Keep in mind that the road to career happiness is usually full of bumps, curves, and tangents rather than a straight, direct path. Waiting for inspiration can be a way of self-sabotaging yourself. As they say in Catalonia, "Caminante, no hay camino. Camino se hace en andar." ("Traveler, there are no paths. Paths are made by walking."). So stop waiting and get walking.

4. **Myth: "Great careers are often a product of luck, being in the right place at the right time."**

Here there is a grain of truth, yet we believe (as did Arnold Palmer) that "the harder you practice, the luckier you get." We call this "managed serendipity"—putting yourself in positions where you are likely to "get lucky." In this regard, most people will benefit from a strategy and a plan.

5. **Myth: "There is one perfect job for me."**

There is usually more "juice" in making the most of where you are, than torturing yourself with the question of whether you are in the right place. We've known people who (despite being in great jobs) always think the grass is greener - this is a guarantee of unhappiness. The simmering dissatisfaction also costs them performance and productivity. Many roads lead to Rome, and you will have to make tradeoffs along the way. Your goal at any stage should be to take the "next best step" that you believe helps you move toward your overall goals.

6. **Myth: "My career has to be linked to my major."**

After a certain age, nobody cares. Even right after college, only one-fourth of graduates work in an area related to their major. Even if you are just starting out, employers care more about the quality of the university and the difficulty of your major (say chemistry versus media studies) than they do about the specifics of your knowledge.

7. **Myth: "It's a numbers game."**

It is and it isn't. You will send out many queries and applications, but well-targeted ones are where the gold is. When one of the coauthors was applying for jobs in his "sweet spot", about 80% of his applications produced an interview. A shotgun approach may not yield even one interview in one hundred applications. Even with targeted applications, you still greatly benefit from having influence over the selection process (we show how in Section 3).

We've looked at current workforce trends and dispelled myths. We now turn to the most helpful set of beliefs about careers—the career mindset.

The 8 Most Important Facets of the Career Mindset

How we think about things determines the results we produce. While the right mindset is no guarantee of short-term results, over the long term, "getting your head right" will produce lifelong benefits. These are the most important aspects of the career mindset:

1. **Career versus job.** Many people use the words "career" and "job" interchangeably, or use "career" more broadly to designate a family of jobs (such as an engineering career) or an industry sector (such as health care). We use the word differently: to describe the portfolio of productive activities over a lifetime, and the development that goes into making those possible. Whatever your job, you need to constantly think about your career, and what the next one-, two-, five-, or ten-year milestones might be.

Further, you have to develop yourself with those milestones and objectives in mind.

2. **The constructed career versus the accidental career.** In (Re)Boot Your Career, we introduce the idea of a "constructed career". Many people fall into their careers and then go with the flow. You can take charge of your own career mindfully by using a foundation of self-knowledge and the employment marketplace. This doesn't mean we ignore serendipity, or refuse to consider other opportunities. A yachtsman may adjust his course for shifting winds and tides, but always begins with a destination in mind.

3. **Align your outsides with your insides.** Developing self-awareness, uncovering your passion, and then aligning what you say about yourself (in interviews, on social media, and in your résumé) with your authentic self creates tremendous power.

4. **Lifelong learning.** Career skill sets are changing rapidly. Whether your formal education stopped with community college, a four-year degree, an MBA, or Ph.D., you must continue to avail yourself of ongoing educational opportunities such as MOOCs (Massive Online Open Courses), webinars, books, conferences, and websites.

5. **Perseverance pays.** It has been said that "overnight success" takes about fifteen years. When we look upon the world of rock-star businesspeople, entrepreneurs, writers, or athletes, we see a snapshot of their lives that can give us the impression they achieved success overnight. The career mindset views the world of work as a marathon, not a sprint.

6. **A growth mindset.** The growth mindset approaches new challenges with the mindset "of a grower, not a knower." The thought "I can't do this" is replaced with "I can't do this yet, but here is an opportunity to learn." Having a negative mindset can limit possibilities for growth and achievement.

7. **Habits help.** Aristotle said that we become what we routinely practice. Having great habits, such as keeping up with professional reading, strategically planning one's time, and cultivating professional relationships means that our professional capabilities stay on an upwards trajectory.

8. **Your online brand.** Today more than just résumés matter. People view your LinkedIn and other professional profiles, and making a positive online impression can create new opportunities. Leveraging social media to propagate your passions and contributions is now common for those serious about their professional development.

Understanding changes in the workforce, unhelpful myths, and the career mindset are the foundation for (re)booting your career. With this macro picture complete, the next section is intensely personal and practical and begins your reboot journey.

SECTION ONE:

The Inside Job – Building Your Foundation

"If you do not find within yourself that which you seek, neither will you find it outside. In you is hidden the treasure of treasures. Know Thyself..."

(The Oracle at Delphi, ca. 350 BCE)

Why is Self-Awareness the Foundation of Career Success?

Each of us will work over 100,000 hours in our lifetimes: is that career to be fulfilling, meaningful, and happy, or drudgery? How we spend those hours is one of the most important decisions we will ever make. Too many people drift along in their careers from lack of tools to make the right choices.

Searching for a job, or choosing a career without deep self-understanding, is a recipe for an unhappy life. Without adequate reflection, we are doomed to repeat earlier mistakes, and when opportunity knocks, we need to answer.

Sometimes we can only find out our likes and dislikes through trial and error. The Wall Street life, with all its material trappings, looked attractive to coauthor Paul at a young age. Eventually, Paul discovered that despite the wealth, the job was deeply unfulfilling. Yet nobody could have dissuaded (and many tried!) him from testing the waters.

To learn from trial and error, however, reflection is essential. This section has tools to help you with that reflection. Reflection should be continual, because as we grow, learn, and change, new dimensions and depths of our "self" emerge that should feature in our deliberations.

While looking inward during this process, we also encourage you to look outward: to the job marketplace. Broaden your reading list to include industry magazines, journals, newspapers, or blogs. This will start to stretch your self-reflection and allow creative ideas to germinate. Read this professional material with your career choice and path in mind, and be aware of workforce trends (like the ones we identified earlier) to make good choices.

Eventually, your enlarged reading list will help you figure out which trends you find meaningful, and which ones you need to explore more deeply.

Stage 1: Beyond the Pursuit of Happiness

We often talk about "happiness" as it relates to our work; unfortunately, we often hear, "I'm not happy." This begs the question: what is happiness, and where and how does it fit into our job?

We all want to be happy, but personal happiness, upon deeper reflection, is too shallow a goal. We suggest that there is "more to happiness than just happiness." The popular notion that our careers should just involve "following your bliss" (an often-heard career mantra) is, we believe, both narcissistic and a recipe for an unworkable career. There is more to it than "bliss," and following "bliss" is a good way to be unhappy.

The concept we endorse is "human flourishing," which comes originally from Greek philosophers, but is now at the core of a discipline called positive psychology that offers a more useful way of understanding happiness.

Flourishing does not dismiss the idea of happiness, but rather adds four more dimensions: spiritual fulfillment, engagement, relationships, and achievement.

> **Spiritual fulfillment**, for us, is not a particular belief system, but rather the notion our work matters, makes a difference, creates value beyond just ourselves, and leaves a legacy.
>
> **Engagement** derives from the work of Hungarian psychologist Czikszentmihalyi (cheek-sent-mee-hi), who studied thousands of people in various professions. His proposal is that when we stretch our talents to capacity, our sense of self dissolves—we become one with the task. This is a feeling of intense absorption, sometimes referred to as "being in the zone" or "in a state of flow."
>
> The **relationships** dimension acknowledges two things. First, that a principal source of well-being (and of health and longevity to boot) is the quality of our relationships. Second, we all have personal "stakeholders": spouses, children, extended family, and communities. Our career choices must serve and respond to more than just our needs. We flourish by giving and receiving from others in our life.
>
> **Achievement** matters to human beings—the sense of pride created by building cathedrals, slaying dragons, and winning at

the game of life. Although each of us defines "winning" differently, it nevertheless is an important part of our psychological makeup.

Finally, there is "**positive affect**," or happiness. While this remains important, it is rightfully placed alongside things that matter more, or equally.

Step 1: Completing the Flourishing questionnaire

With a clear understanding of **flourishing,** complete the following short questionnaire using a 1 to 5 scale (1 being "strongly disagree" and 5 being "strongly agree"):

Dimensions of human flourishing	Score (1-5)
I feel, that through my work, I am contributing to something worthwhile	
I lead a purposeful and meaningful life	
My career is aligned with my values and mission	
Spiritual fulfillment	
I am fully engaged and interested in my daily activities	
I am constantly learning and continually challenged	
I sometimes lose track of time doing work I enjoy	
Engagement	
My work relationships are supportive, rich, and rewarding	
I actively contribute to the happiness and well-being of others	
I feel respected and valued at work	
Relationships	
I continually achieve success	
I accomplish important goals I set for myself	
I am competent and capable in the activities that matter to me	
Achievements	
I am optimistic about my future	
I look forward to Mondays (more generally, to working)	
I am happy at work most of the time	
Positive affect	
TOTAL	

Step 2: Scoring the questionnaire

Add up your scores to each statement; the maximum score is 75 (strongly agreed with each statement) and the minimum score would be 15 (strongly disagreed with each statement). Your overall score will provide you with a general flourishing level; however, what will probably be more interesting are your sub-scores in each category, because they suggest what might be missing.

Step 3: Reflecting and journaling

Exploring your individual and overall scoring from the flourishing questionnaire, reflect on the following questions:

> Which scores are much lower than I would like them to be, and how do I feel about that?
>
> Is there a particular category I am concerned with (spiritual fulfillment, engagement, relationships, achievement, and/or positive effect), and how do I feel about that?
>
> For each specific score that concerns you, reflect on the specific circumstances that lead you to score yourself that way. Capture those specifics and reflect on what changes you can make to improve your score.

Step 4: Talking to two or three confidants

Write their names in your journal and email them right now (while the iron is hot) asking for 30 minutes of their time over a meal, coffee, or another favorite beverage. Explore with them what you are discovering. This will help you clarify and cement it, perhaps validate your thinking, and provide you with the motivation to go on.

Stage 2: Components of a Rewarding Career

We hope that, after Stage 1, you now will think beyond the age-old question "Are you happy?" The Flourishing questionnaire should help you self-reflect on what elements in your life aren't working for you as well as you would like.

There is more to career choice than just flourishing. Consider the model below:

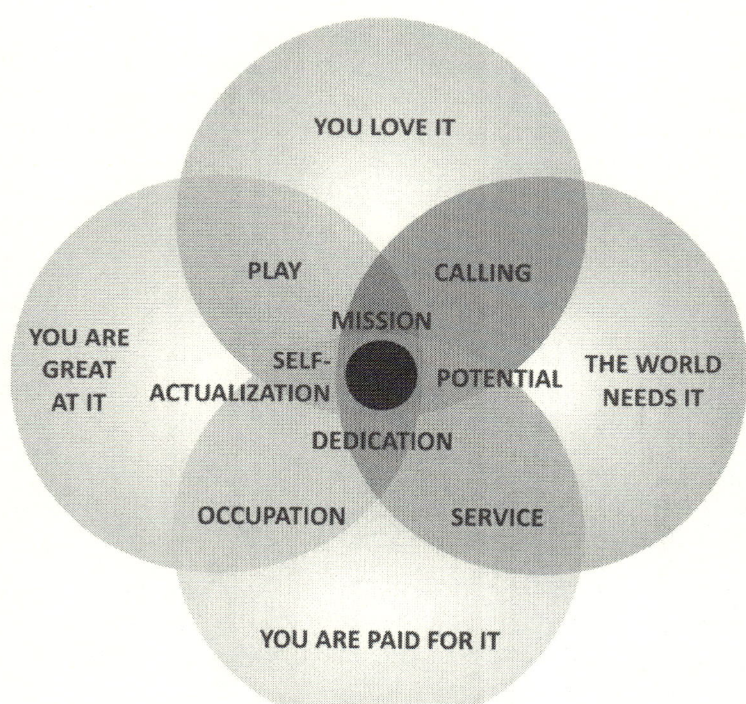

• PURPOSE

This model incorporates some of the ideas from flourishing, but is broader. The important elements are:

The world needs it: This includes spouses, children, parents, communities and places you care about, and your commitment to issues bigger than you (peace, sustainability, liberty). This dimension brings in both practical concerns (such as living in a good place for kids to grow up), and spiritual concerns (serving something greater than yourself). Where this intersects with the dimension "You love it" is your "calling."

You love it: This is the answer to the question, "If money were never a concern, how would you spend your time?" What activities give you the most joy? Where this intersects with "You are great at it" could be called "play."

You are great at it: When your cousin assaults your eardrums playing his violin, you realize that some people enjoy things regardless of talent. You may also be good at things that you don't enjoy. This introduces the dimensions of skills and competence into your career choices: where do you excel? The intersection of this with "You are paid for it" is called your "occupation," or "calling."

You are paid for it: The childish fantasy is if you just do what you love ("follow your bliss"), the money will follow. It is more realistic to weigh and balance secular concerns (like money) with spiritual concerns (such as your calling). The intersection of this with "The world needs it" is called "being of service."

Step 1: Reflecting and journaling

In your journal, reflect on the following questions:

If money were not an object, what would I do?

Whose needs are important as I consider career opportunities?

What greater causes do I wish to support?

Where is my skill "sweet spot?"

In which areas could I be world-class with sufficient effort?

What are my financial needs?

Which of my skills are in greatest demand?

Stage 3: Personality—How Am I Wired?

Our personality begins to emerge before our first birthday, and although we grow and change over time, many personality aspects remain hardwired and stable. "She's the kind of person who is fun to be with," or "Charlie's a daredevil."

Hippocrates, around 400 BCE, first speculated that there were four different personality types. Since then, efforts to categorize people have produced more than 1,000 different personality questionnaires. We chose the PAVF Work-Styles tool from those because is particularly relevant in our modern work environment and is easy to work with.

Step 1: Completing the PAVF Work-Styles Profiling Survey

To assess yourself, rank each of the horizontal sets of four words. '3' represents the word that resembles you the most, '0' represents the word that resembles you the least, and '2' and '1' are in between. Make sure each line contains only one instance of each of number, and do not use the same number twice on the same line.

PAVF Survey

Example:

Involved	*0*	*Cautious*	*2*	*Colorful*	*3*	*Cooperative*	*1*

Involved		Cautious		Colorful		Cooperative	
Direct		Detailing		Charismatic		Receptive	
Doing		Watching		Brainstorming		Empathetic	
Aware		Evaluator		Risk-taker		Accepting	
Impatient		Logical		Questioning		Helpful	
Active		Observing		Different		Interactive	
Pragmatic		Reflecting		Future-oriented		Warm	
Winning		Thorough		Conceptual		By consensus	
Rational		Reserved		Ideas person		Gather information	
No-nonsense		Careful		Outgoing		Personable	

Totals

P	Total:		A	Total:		V	Total:		F	Total:	

Sum of totals must equal 60. If the sum does not equal 60, go back through the survey results line by line, checking your addition and whether you scored yourself correctly per the above instructions.

Step 2: Scoring your survey

You should now have four numbers that add up to 60 (for example, P = 12, A = 15, V=20, and F = 13). Again, if the four numbers don't add up exactly to 60, double-check your score and addition.

Most of us are dominant in one or two of these work styles; some may be dominant in three; however, it is impossible to be dominant in all four, as we shall soon see.

Determining dominant and secondary work styles

We define "dominant" (as in, "I am a dominant P") when your score is **18 or above** and "secondary" when your score is **15 or above**. We write out the work-style types from left to right, starting with P, then A, then V, and finally F. We express dominant work style(s) in uppercase letters, and secondary work style(s) in lowercase letters.

Thus, in our example of P = 12, A = 15, V=20, and F = 13, this person has a secondary work style of A (at 15), and a primary dominance of V (scoring 20). We would write that as aV.

Here are the descriptions of each PAVF type:

P = Producer

The Producer has the drive and discipline necessary to produce real results. Impatient, active, and always busy, the **Producer** has little time for idle chitchat. Direct and to the point, they are behind-the-scenes movers and shakers. (Example words: *Results-oriented, extroverted, strong-willed, direct, decisive, task-oriented, domineering, impatient, sometimes insensitive and short-tempered*).

A = Analyzer

The Analyzer ensures the rules are in place and in effect, and plans are made and adhered to. Precise and accurate, the **Analyzer** creates methods and procedures to make sure the details are right. Organized and logical, they clean up other people's carelessness. (Example words: *Logical, thorough, disciplined, fact-oriented, withdrawn, quiet, reclusive, sometimes perceived as dull, avoids taking risks*).

V = Visionary

The Visionary is an "ideas person" who seeks to improve, always asking "why?" or "why not?" A dreamer, planner, and a schemer, the **Visionary** leads others to ideas that they would not pursue on their own. Success of a Visionary requires both creativity and risk. (Example words: *Enthusiastic, outgoing, persuasive, fun-loving, spontaneous, relationship-oriented, sometimes unfocused, tendency to generalize, occasionally has verbal assaults and irrational behavior*).

F = Friend

The Friend is a people-oriented person, everyone's pal who thrives on peacemaking and teamwork. Unmistakably pleasant and charming, amiable and empathetic, the **Friend** is cooperative and helpful, and holds groups together. (Example words: *Devoted, dependable, loyal, hardworking, persevering, cooperative, sometimes indecisive, people pleaser*).

Step 3: Understanding your PAVF profile

Examine your scores from the profiling survey; assess their relevance to the way you think you are. There are a few general trends:

Most people have some in each category.

Most people have one or two clear preferences.

A few people are nearly equal in all areas.

There is no good or bad for any particular profile. What matters most is the *fit* between your preferences and the kind of work you do. While people can adapt; that is, learn detail-oriented skills (A), even if they prefer big-picture thinking (V), preferences tend to be hardwired and hence longer lasting.

In our work with this survey, we occasionally hear from clients that as a dominant V or F they feel somewhat slighted, because they think their scores imply they "don't do the real work of Ps and As." There are two insights into this worth mentioning:

1. The language in most workplaces is dominant P (Producer) and A (Analyzer) language, and so those work styles are more engaged. Most supervisors give instructions as, "I want you to do this (P) and do it this way (A)." This tends to skew people toward overemphasizing their P and A components and underutilizing their V and F aspects. Consequently, as a dominant V or F, you may feel underappreciated (or misunderstood) in your workplace.

2. Think of your dominant work style(s) as the main filter through which you interpret the work world. When someone assigns you a new task, if you are a dominant P, you immediately think, "**What** results do we want?" The dominant A thinks, "**How** am I being asked to do this?" The dominant V thinks, "**Why** are we doing it this way?" Finally, the dominant F thinks, "**Who** is involved and impacted by this?" A dominant F isn't ignoring the what, why, and how aspects—just that their primary filter is who.

The table on the next page illustrates each personality type's characteristics.

	Producer (P)	Analyzer (A)	Visionary (V)	Friend (F)
Typical Characteristics	Task & results oriented, extroverted, strong-willed, direct, decisive, domineering, impatient	Analytical, detail-oriented, logical, factual, thorough, patient, disciplined, withdrawn, quiet, reclusive, controlling	Creative, flexible, outgoing, enthusiastic, persuasive, fun-loving, spontaneous, short attention span, makes verbal assaults	Amiable, devoted, dependable, loyal, hardworking, cooperative, indecisive
General Character	Busy	Orderly	Has Ideas	Cooperative
Fears	Not getting it done	Chaos	Not being appreciated	Conflict
Weaknesses	Becomes a bottleneck	Inaction paralysis	Takes too many risks	Wishy-washy
Perspective of P (how P views others)	Sees another P as competition	Thinks A implements too many rules and obstacles in the way	Views V as lacking focus on results	Views F as dawdling, in the pursuit of consensus
Perspective of A (how A views others)	Views P as short- circuiting process	Views another A as a good, silent worker	Perceives V as a loose cannon	Considers F too friendly and soft
Perspective of V (how V views others)	Thinks P has no idea of the big picture	Views A as too constricting	Sees another V as wanting too much credit	Thinks F has no original ideas
Perspective of F (how F views others)	Finds P to be too impatient, too hard	Feels that A is too factual	Views V as too avant-garde	Believes that another F offers a chance for real conversation
Communicates	Need-to-know basis	By focusing on details	Verbally mainly, rarely in writing	With many others
Appreciates	Hard workers	People under control	Those who respect me	Those who get along
Likes	Getting results	Organizing	Winning peer approval	Being nice

Generalized career choices should surface from an understanding of your PAVF makeup. There are two general streams for career progression: Stream #1 is management, which is mostly about getting things done though other people. Stream #2 is specialization, becoming an expert in your field. Here are some general considerations for each:

Management

Managers need to deliver; that is, to get results, so a strong P makes this a more natural feat. If you have the desire to manage but lack a strong P, then you must augment your P by:

Playing a stronger **P** role (which requires determination and adds some stress to your life);

Creating systems and tools (checklists, tables, etc.) that make the **P** come forth in your processes;

Shadowing a colleague strong in **P**, who oversees the **"P"** aspect of the job (i.e., getting immediate results).

Another alternative is to avoid leading a large group or an extremely critical project. Limit yourself to managing smaller groups that your size of **P** will allow you to control successfully and naturally.

The specialist

The specialist achieves success by attention to detail and a passion for a subject, namely taking advantage of a high-innate **A**. If you want to be an expert but lack a strong **A**, then you must supplement your **A** by:

Playing a stronger **A** role (which requires determination and adds some stress to your life).

Shadowing a colleague strong in **A**, who contributes strongly to the **"A"** aspect of the job (i.e., the fine details).

The innovator

To bring forward new ideas and new processes requires the talents of a **V**. These types of roles are usually in public and private sector research foundations, such as universities, policy think tanks, and R&D labs of large private sector companies.

The caregiver

If you have a strong **F**, you want to take care of all people, both known to you and strangers. Here, a role as a counselor, coach, human resource person, trainer, or society advocate would fit well. Because of their concern for people and social causes, dominant **Fs** are often attracted to the social sector (nonprofits).

The salesperson

As a person who likes deliver results (and quickly), a **P** is a natural salesperson. However, to have a successful long-term sales career requires more than **P**. Sales also involve looking for creative solutions to customer issues, namely **V**. Successful sales also requires looking after many details, namely **A**. Often the salesperson is **PV**, and is supported by a resource (sales support) that has a strong **A**.

The entrepreneur

The entrepreneur must possess a strong **P**, an urge to get things done. Combined with a strong **V**, a desire to implement ideas creates a **PV**. Running your own business requires selfless dedication, and the unrelenting drive of **P** combined with self-confidence and the numerous ideas of **V**.

The researcher

To create new ideas, new processes, and new thoughts requires the natural talents of a **V**, as well as attention to details (**A**). Thus, a researcher probably should display a natural **AV** talent. This is a dilemma because **A** and **V** are a conflicting pairing. Since V is necessary for innovation, the combination for research should be **aV**, namely an emphasis on the **V** aspect (dominant **V**, with secondary **A**).

Step 4: Reflecting and journaling

Take 15 to 20 minutes now to reread the PAVF material and jot down any insights it provides about you, your current work roles, and your relationships with others. Ask yourself the following questions:

> Do my score and the associated behaviors and typical careers described make sense to me?
>
> How has this shifted how I think about myself?

Is there a link between my “flourishing” and how closely my previous roles match up to this profile?

Do I feel the need for work more closely aligned with my profile strength(s)?

Stage 4: How Do I Describe Myself?

In the previous PAVF section, each of the four work styles (P, A, V, and F) are associated with words that describe various ways of operating; the mental imagery created when you consider each work style varies greatly.

What we want you to do now is go deeper in your word selection and choose specific words that resonate with who you are and how you operate. You will then carry those words over through the rest of the book to build powerful and accurate imagery about how you accomplish things and add value.

The point of this exercise is to help you develop an authentic brand, so don't choose a word you "wished" described you (or how you want others to see you!), rather than how you really are. The whole point here is to be truthful to yourself as to who you really are, and use that description to tell a compelling story. We refer to these as your anchor words—or more usefully, your evolving **descriptors**—as they are part of the foundational structure that will help you anchor your story and value proposition (brand).

Step 1: Creating a first cut word pile

As you come across powerful words that affect you, record these words in your journal. You will be reducing and refining these words in other exercises, so for now focus on compiling meaningful words. Here are some easy places to start:

1. First, you can go back to your PAVF Work-Styles Profiling Survey and circle words that stand out to you from the survey. These are usually words with a score of "3" and are often in your highest-rated columns.

2. Next, review the PAVF descriptions, and again circle the words you find meaningful from the various descriptor words.

3. Now scan through the words in the following table; again, circle the words you believe best embody who you are and how you operate (both in work and play):

Competitive	Honest	Respectful
Composed	Human relations, belief in	Responsible
Confident	Humorous	Results-oriented
Conscientious	Iconoclast (goes against traditions)	Reviewing
Consensus building	Idealistic	Risk taker
Controlling	Imaginative	Scheduling before acting
Convincing	Impulsive	Selling ideas
Cooperative	Individualist	Setting strategy
Coordinating	Influencing	Sharing
Courageous	Innovative	Shy; Reserved
Creative	Insightful	Small group preference
Crisis management	Inspecting	Sociable
Dealing with Pressure	Integrity	Spontaneous
Decisive	Intuitive	Strategizing
Delegating	Inventive	Strong-willed
Dependable	Leadership, assuming readily	Structured
Designing	Liaison	Sympathetic
Detailed and in depth	Listening	Tactful
Determined	Logical	Team player
Devoted	Loyal	Tenacious
Diligent	Maintain as a matter of course	Thorough
Diplomatic	Mechanical	Thoughtful of others
Directing	Mediating	Time management
Disciplined	Meticulous	Tireless
Discovering	Monitoring	Traditional
Discreet	Motivating others	Trusting
Drive	Objective	Understanding of others
Easygoing	Observing	Visionary
Efficient	Optimistic	Warm
Empathetic	Organized	Well-read
Energetic	Overcautious as viewed by others	Willing

If there are other words you like, don't hesitate to add them to your word pile. The point here is not to be reductive, but to be expansive and brainstorm significant words. You will go through them later and whittle them down to size.

You probably now have 25 or so words. If you have fewer, that's fine. If you have more, go back through your words and try to eliminate similar words or choose the word more meaningful to you. Write this list of words out in your journal so you have it handy for future exercises.

Step 2: Doing the career ad exercise

The purpose of this exercise is twofold: the first is to identify further meaningful words; the second is to expand your horizons toward interesting career opportunities. Again, record this work in your journal.

Begin to read want ads from any source: local newspapers, online job boards, out-of-town periodicals, etc.;

Cut or print out any ads with jobs that appeal to you, regardless of whether or not you are qualified or interested in their geographic location;

Highlight the words within the ads that appealed to you;

When you have gathered anywhere from 10 to 20 ads, summarize a list of the words that appealed to you the most and add them to your existing word pile.

Keep a copy of these ads handy with the highlighted words. You will review them again in the next section of this book when you develop your *Opportunity Sought* statement. There you will have a chance to reflect on the jobs that appeal to you and why they appeal to you, irrespective of whether or not you are qualified for them.

Step 3: Consolidating your first cut list of Descriptors

By now, you probably have 30 to 50 words in your word pile written in your journal. You can take some time now to clean up the list a little more and remove more duplicates and weaker words.

Once you are comfortable with your Descriptors and each word resonates with you, put your journal aside and take a break from your word pile. You'll revisit this exercise later in the book.

Stage 5: Unpacking Your Backpack

One of the main tenets of coaching is that clients already have the experience (whether that is work experience, life experience, or any other experiences). Part of the coach's job is to help bring that experience to the surface and help the client reframe and understand it better, giving the client the self-confidence to appreciate his or her own strengths more and take positive action going forward.

Think of your young self. A family member probably dropped you off at your first school. Undoubtedly, you proudly sported a bright new backpack, which then slowly filled up with your homework assignments and personal mementos over the following weeks and months. As you progressed through school and life, you added more experiences to that metaphorical backpack—a school project here, a life experience there, your first volunteer assignment, a summer job, your first full-time job, and so on.

What we rarely—if ever—do is to actually stop at some point, sit down, and empty out that backpack to see what we have collected and how our collection can help us understand our path. Most of us don't have the time or interest to really reflect on how we got here and where we want to go next. Typically, if we do need to reflect on a recent experience (such as updating our résumés with recent roles), we just pull out the immediate "stuff" sitting on top of our metaphorical backpack. We then think about it for a few minutes, write up a quick statement about those roles, and add it to our résumé. We do not dig very deeply into our backpack because, frankly, who has the time and the interest to do that work?

Since you are reading this book, we're assuming that you have both the time and the interest for this right now. Now is the time to sit down and unpack your backpack.

Step 1: Listing your work and life accomplishments

Pull out your journal and write a list of about 12 personal and professional accomplishments, even the nontraditional ones. The work-related ones are usually straightforward; however, sometimes the personal and nontraditional ones provide an insight into your character.

For example, moving away from home on your own under difficult circumstances might have felt like a major accomplishment to you.

Perhaps you valued your work on a recent committee. Alternatively, it might be supporting a friend through a rough patch, or building a tree house when you were very young. (Even millennials, with fewer years of formal work experience, should generate a dozen or so of these.)

Now write a few-sentence description of each, using bullet points if that is easier.

Step 2: Correlating your descriptors with your accomplishments

You now have two different lists: one contains a short description of up to 12 top accomplishments; the other is your pile of words.

Now go through each of your accomplishments, look at your list of words, and circle the ones that you believe were critical components of your success. To prepare for this activity, start by neatly writing out your words on a single sheet of paper, and then make up to 12 copies of that page (one copy for each accomplishment). Now:

> Number each of your accomplishments from #1 to #12;
>
> Grab your first copy of your word sheet, mark it in the corner as #1, and then reading and rereading accomplishment #1, go through your word list and ask yourself: "To accomplish this, was it critical that I was ____________?" If the answer is yes, then circle that word. Repeat for each word on your page. After a few minutes of this, you should have about 8 to 10 words circled on your word page #1.
>
> Now, grab another word sheet, mark it as #2, and go through accomplishment #2 and ask yourself the same question for every word.
>
> Complete this exercise for each of your accomplishments. This exercise will probably take you an hour minimum, and possibly up to 90 minutes.

At the end of this exercise, you will have a deeper understanding of the characteristics that contributed to your accomplishments. You are beginning to encapsulate your life in a few words.

Step 3: Reducing your word pile

Now go back through your 12 word sheets and add up which words you used the most. On a clean page in your journal, under the title Key

Descriptors, write down the words you circled most frequently, starting with the most circled word through the list. Record the top seven to nine words circled.

Look through your new list and old list. Are there any words that didn't make the short list, but you feel strongly about them and aren't ready to discard yet?

Make another list of four to five additional words you feel strongly about but didn't make the first **Key Descriptors** cut.

Keep them separate, but write them out in your journal to reflect on later.

In this section, we are selecting words to use in all our communications about our career. Although seemingly simple, it is worth taking your time and reflecting as you are doing it. Now let's test these words with our confidants.

Step 4: Getting feedback from trusted sources

The fastest, most direct way to test and refine your **Key Descriptors** is to reengage your trusted friends and confidants from previous exercises. Sitting down with your confidants (individually or as a group), ask them to help you validate your list(s). At this point, you will have up to 14 words (if you made a second list of runner-up words) and you want your friends to help you whittle that down to 8 or 9 words. Hopefully your friends will ask you to elaborate, which will deepen the quality of your insights.

During these sessions, take detailed notes in your journal. These conversations will provide all kinds of raw input for you to reflect upon and build on in subsequent exercises.

Stage 6: Declaring Your Mission, Vision, and Values

Until now, the exercises in this section were anchored in the here-and-now (your PAVF work style), or in recalling your history (unpacking your backpack). These provide the foundation for making career decisions more aligned with your gifts and passions.

Now we are going to take a "10,000-foot view" of your life, and challenge you to envision the future and declare what you are committed to in life and work. There are three parts shown in the diagram below.

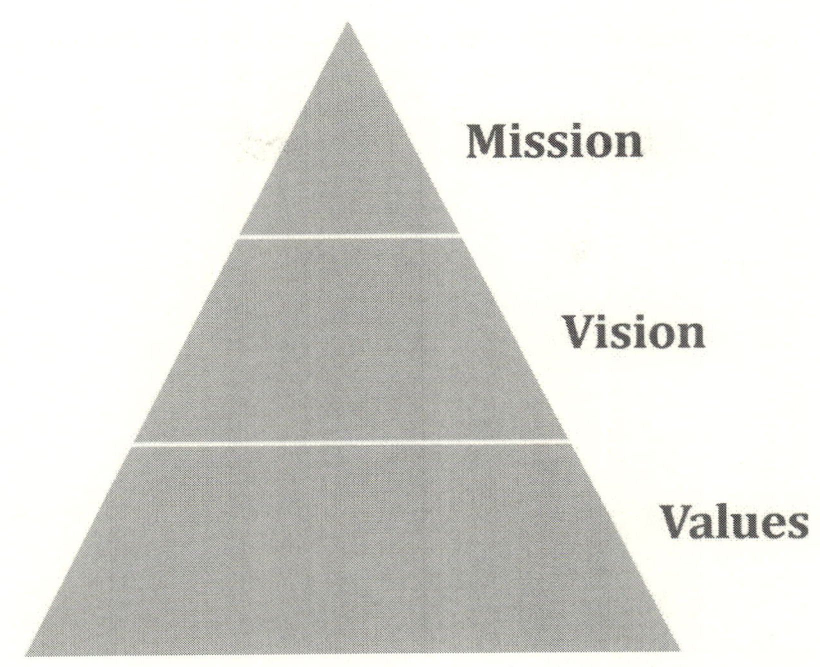

The point of the mission statement

A mission statement describes what you want to contribute to life. It does three things: establishes a focus for your life, gives meaning to the things that you do, and provides a context for making decisions. Your mission statement may be a single sentence, or an entire paragraph; however, we counsel simplicity, inspiration, and focus.

Here are some examples of mission statements you can use to reflect on what your own mission statement might be.

"I heal people through the practice of medicine and the quality of the medical and emotional care they receive. My general practice focuses holistically on well-being and illness prevention. But mostly wellness and prosperity begin at home, and my husband and children feel my care most deeply."

"I elevate the most important conversations in the world by writing, teaching, and bringing creative ideas where they are needed. My work integrates science, philosophy, and business, transforms lives and organizations, and helps shape a better future for the planet. When not

doing the work I love, I'm raising two amazing boys and living a full, passionate life."

"I help people get the most from technology, and support my communities and family passionately."

"I bring all of myself to my role as an administrative assistant, growing my skills each year and being an example to my boss of a stress-free, balanced, and organized life. In three years, my legal assistant qualification will allow me to make a bigger difference and help me better provide for my children. Away from career and home, I serve the community through helping with political campaigns and working on the PTA."

Step 1: Creating a mission statement

You may already be living your mission, perhaps without ever having expressed it succinctly. View this exercise as a compelling way of expressing who you already are. To begin creating your mission statement, reflect on the following questions and jot down the answers in your journal:

> What do I intend to do about opportunities before me?
>
> Where will those opportunities take me?
>
> What careers inspired me when I was young? (Maybe I can't be an astronaut anymore, but what about being an astronaut was exciting or inspiring?)
>
> How do I want to serve others?
>
> What capabilities do I love using?
>
> What makes me unique?

The role of the vision

A vision is a specific, current description of your future. The timescale for a vision is typically five to fifteen years. It should do two things: inspire you and others you share it with, and point you toward some specific goals. We believe that a vision, like a mission statement, should be inspirational and aspirational.

In our experience as coaches, most people think too small. Most people overestimate what they can *do in a day, and grossly underestimate* what they can do in a decade. *Your vision has to be specific, set a clear destination, and be achievable.*

> *"I will be a recognized authority in digital video compression and an accomplished C++ programmer by 2020."*
>
> *"I will have a photography portfolio that is found in at least four local galleries, and be selling at least $20,000 of prints through my online business by 2020."*
>
> *"I will be a sought-out executive facilitator by the international SME marketplace by 2025."*
>
> *"I will be the general manager of a multinational company within the next five years."*

Step 2: Constructing your vision

Open your journal and jot down five to six ideas of what you think your vision statement might be. Don't over think this or be overly critical about your ideas; write down the first few things that come to mind without judging whether they are believable at this point.

Set out a timeline on the vertical axis of a page of your journal, starting in one-to two-year increments, and moving along to five-year increments. Then, along the horizontal, place a column for career, for family, for education, and other meaningful pursuits. How will success unfold over those years along the different dimensions of your life (career, family, education, etc.)? What specific milestones along the way will be most important and meaningful?

Building on these ideas, write down your grand but realistic ambition for yourself. It should reflect what you envision five or ten years down the road. This may be difficult for some; simply do the best you can. Lay out the long-distance view of your life, something clear for you to strive for, within your profession and your life. Remember to include numbers and specificity to help assure reality.

Spend about a week refining your vision. Revise your thoughts as needed, and take notes in your journal as you work and rework this exercise. One of Paul's other books, *Reboot Your Life*, has several tools, and there are many other free resources online.

How values fit into the picture

We have broader values than just career values. Career values tell us something about the work we enjoy, but values such as sustainability, fairness, or learning tell us how we derive meaning from the work we choose to do (one of the dimensions of flourishing).

Especially in times of change, it is important that we have values as a constant. In stressful moments, we can fall back on our values to answer life- or business-related questions. You must be both guardian and practitioner of those values. Starting with your personal values will lead to a final direction. Values do not change very much with time, while one's mission and vision will probably evolve greatly. How to behave (values) will remain the most constant of the three mission components.

Values answer the question "How do I want to act (consistent with my mission, along the path toward achieving my vision)?" Values are not results or strategies; they are foundational and part of your belief system.

Roundness	Collaboration	Integrity	Diversity	Respect
Achievement	Innovation	Honesty	Reflection	Stewardship
Collegiality	Accountability	Culturally competent	Social justice	Aspirational
Contribution	Teamwork	Community	Ambitious	Flexibility
Inclusion	Concern	Optimization	Lifelong learning	Equitable
Evidence-based	Customer service	Sustainability	Transparency	Balance
Responsibility	Administratively competent	Roundness	Leveling the playing field	Seekers of excellence
Quality	Curious	Resilience	Engagement	Care, caring
Inspirational	Strategically minded	Action oriented	Efficient	Responsive
Environmental	Familial	Balanced	Character	Supportive
Engagement	Passion	Inclusive	Equanimous	Professionalism
Dedication	Roundness	Ethical	Agility	Cooperation

The word list (previous page) contains dozens of possible value statements that might be compelling to you. Similar to your previous word pile exercise, identify a few words that you believe represent your core values.

Step 3: Declaring your values

In your journal, record your ideas about what your core values are:

From the word list, circle five to ten words that jump out at you, in both a work and life context;

Narrow these down to four to six words that you feel strongly about;

If you think of additional words that are not on the list, jot these down also.

Examining the words you have chosen above, reflect on the following questions in your journal:

What does each word mean to you? Write each word out in a separate sentence that reflects its underlying importance to you.

For each word, write a short example of how you live that value in your everyday actions.

Write down a few thoughts about what you hope you would do if you found yourself in a situation where someone was demonstrating the opposite of your chosen value.

Step 4: Sharing this work with your confidants

Once you feel you have a solid working draft of your mission, vision, and values, share them with your confidants. Make sure you capture their feedback—these detailed notes of their observations will be useful to review as you work through the rest of this book.

When you are comfortable with the various components of the mission, vision, and values that make up a personal mission statement, you can combine them into a powerful paragraph that becomes a key aspect of your story (which you will develop more fully in the next section of this book). Here is an example of how the mission, vision, and values work comes together:

Example: Mission, vision, values

(My Purpose)

My mission is to help people:

- Communicate effectively
- Identify core issues and work together to discover solutions
- Streamline efforts toward effective and efficient resolution
- Work on relationships
- Organize themselves

My vision is to:

- Develop a wide-ranging presence and reputation for excellence in assisting people, and by 2020 have a certification or position that recognizes that excellence
- Foster positive international relations and have a positive impact in the global community as evidenced by a paper, journal, book, or tangible item by the year 2022

My core values include:

- Integrity: To be accountable for my words and actions
- Autonomy: To work from a basic level of mutual trust and respect
- Analysis: To enhance, improve, streamline; to help people make a difference

Having completed the values exercises, you will have a clearer sense of what matters to you both professionally and personally. You will specifically call on this exercise as part of your filter-design work in Section 3. Before we get there; however, you are going to put your story together in Section 2.

SECTION ONE: Recap

This section has been all about helping you figure out who you are and what truly matters to you—essentially, the "inside job" of deep reflection:

You captured a baseline of your **current flourishing level** (an improved expression over happiness, which is often too one-dimensional), and reflected specifically on what you want to improve;

You completed our **PAVF Work-Styles Profiling Survey** and developed a clearer sense of your dominant strengths (some combination of Producer, Analyzer, Visionary, and/or Friend);

From your PAVF profile, you **selected powerful words** you felt strongly about and can use to describe yourself. You added some "real-world" examples to that list by studying career ads and adding some of their words that you noticed;

You "unpacked your backpack," and from that exercise captured up to **a dozen of your accomplishments** of which you are particularly proud;

You combined your accomplishments and word pile (we called it "correlating"), and from there reduced your word pile to a much more manageable list that became your **Key Descriptors**;

You **tested the Key Descriptors** with some trusted friends, and took copious notes about their feedback;

Finally, you reflected on your **mission, vision, and values**, and pulled them together into a solid first draft of your personal mission statement.

Well done—you've set a really strong foundation for the work still to come in the next two sections!

SECTION TWO:
DEVELOPING A PERSONAL BRAND – YOUR COMPELLING VALUE STORY

So, What Can You Do for Me?

All hiring managers—regardless of industry, company, or other distinguishing factor—want a new hire that solves problems and gets results. Yet many people are not good at explaining how they will solve those problems and obtain those results—and through doing so, making their prospective boss' life easier. Interviewees often present themselves as a bucket of skills and competencies. Hiring managers have to "connect the dots" between that bucket of skills and the results they want. This may leave them impressed with your qualifications, but in some doubt as to the usefulness of the potential hire: you!

The more we can describe the results we produce for people and employers and how we produce them through interviews and written material, the more attractive we are as candidates.

This section takes you through a series of exercises that will help you build and hone your own story about how you add value through your capabilities and experiences. Moreover, you'll be able to describe clearly what that "fit" looks like in terms the reader will understand. Specifically, you'll construct:

A concise, compelling two-page résumé, but in a quick format that addresses the main questions on a reader's/interviewer's mind;

A master résumé (three to four pages) from which to build two-page versions for specific opportunities;

Your biography and tagline (for your résumé, LinkedIn, and other public profiles);

Your LinkedIn profile;

A personalized social media strategy.

The Uses and Abuses of Résumés

In today's competitive employment world, creating a polished, impressive résumé is just the beginning. However, when correctly constructed, it's a distillation of what is special and desirable about you as an employee. Sending out a strong résumé isn't enough, as it is competing alongside hundreds of others. A great résumé is necessary, but not sufficient, for success today. We'll talk about that more in Section 3 (The Outside Job: Modern Job-Hunting Skills).

The format and length constraints of the standard résumé will force you to condense your story, while retaining and linking all the elements together in a strong message. The narrative must be coherent, and your transitions must describe the trajectory of your career in such a way that the position you seek is an obvious next challenge.

We recommend several counterintuitive ideas in this section that run contrary to orthodoxy.

1. The first idea relates to tailoring your résumé for each position. Don't! We recommend a master résumé you modify infrequently. Résumés sent to interested parties will have modifications to the first section (Opportunity Sought) and your story (your brand, experience, accomplishments, and capabilities), but the core of your story should be in-depth in your master résumé.

2. Our second counterintuitive idea is to see your résumé as a story, with a central character (you) and a fascinating plot (your career to date). You discovered more about your authentic self in Section 1; sell those unique capabilities during the application process!

3. Our third idea relates to how to structure your résumé. We tell you how to focus on readers and how they view your résumé.

This section will help you put those ideas together to create a résumé that stands out and expresses your true self.

Selling the Character in Your Story – You!

In section 1, we used the PAVF Work-Styles Profiling Survey to help you understand "the real you" at work—your preferences, work style, strengths, and weaknesses. We recommend you use the PAVF language and your descriptors in your résumé. The PAVF styles, as you recall, are:

P – Producer: one who produces, is driven, disciplined, persistent, hardworking, and direct;

A – Analyzer: one who analyzes and plans ahead, is thorough, organized, logical, and detail-oriented;

V – Visionary: one who foresees improvement, is an ideas-person, risky, creative, innovative, curious, and one dream ahead;

F – Friend: friendly, empathetic, embodies cooperation, and people-oriented.

Get out your journal and review your PAVF profile. For example, if you have established that you are a PV, you can emphasize one main characteristic of each work style to describe yourself (review your **Key Descriptor**s list). For example, let's use "results-oriented" from P and "creative problem solving" from V.

"I'm driven to get results (P) and find creative new solutions to problems (V)."

This is effectively your "plotline"—your brand, emphasis, and focus. You do these things well because they come naturally to you. This is the real you. Stick to that message: it is succinct and states clearly and accurately who you are. Let there be no doubt. Your close friends and family will recognize this about you already, but now you want to show your authentic self and your strengths to prospective employers.

Stage 1: Building your Résumé Step by Step

The traditional résumé structure makes readers work too hard. Hiring managers and recruiters have to infer what you can do for them from generic objective statements, your education, and job history.

They don't care about this information yet. Right now, they only care if you can serve their business or organizational needs. This makes the traditional résumé format ineffective. Busy recruiters and hiring managers may scan your résumé and quickly discard it if the story of how you (uniquely) produce results does not grab them instantly. We want to make the reader's life easy, capture his or her attention with a "hook," and build emotional connection and interest.

Our recommended structure addresses their questions (what they really want to know) in the order they want them answered.

Is this person a fit for our business needs right now? (This is the **Opportunity Sought** statement.)

How do I know this person can do what he or she claims? (This is the **Capabilities** section.)

What else has this person accomplished? (This is the **Accomplishments** section.)

Has this person done similar jobs like this before? (This is the **Professional Experience** section.)

With these questions in mind, here is our recommended résumé format:

Corresponding section	Section objective
Contact Details	Provide the best way to contact you for an interview.
Opportunity Sought	Capture the reader's initial interest.
Accomplishments	Allow the reader to scan your résumé and see your previous successes. This section also discloses achievements and results and reveals your true personality.
Professional Experience	Supply additional details such as your employment history, education, awards, etc.
Personal Information	Hobbies, interests, family (if you choose to include that).

We recommend everyone use this two-page format, whether you are early in your career or have 30 years of experience.

At the top of the first page, employers find out about the **future**—that is, whether you can solve their business problems. This is your **Opportunity Sought** statement.

Next, they want to know about **now** (what you currently have that will deliver future results). You address that in your Capabilities and **Accomplishments**. By infusing your first page with strong accomplishments that highlight your Key Descriptors (which we developed in Section 1), the reader is starting to build an emotional connection with you.

On page two, highlight your **past** in the **Professional Experience** section. Readers only care about your potential value. Your work history serves as evidence that reinforces your **Opportunity Sought** and Capabilities.

Now we will help you create an excellent résumé step by step. Even though the **Accomplishments** section is after the **Opportunity Sought** and **Capabilities** statements in the résumé layout, we recommend you finalize this section first. Most people find it easier to recall previous achievements, and as they build and edit those into results-specific statements, they gain confidence in their abilities. This makes writing their Opportunity Sought statement easier.

Step 1: Showcasing your accomplishments

An Accomplishments statement should have three components, all working together to communicate what you did, how you did it, and the results you generated. Think of these as three strings you can tie together:

1. "Because of my basic work style (highlighting one of your **Key Descriptors**)..."
2. "When tasked to do the following (**what you did** or worked on)..."
3. "I was able to generate these **quantified results** (meaningful to the organization—the **value**)..."

We're now going to use the Accomplishment statements you developed in Section 1. If you are early in your career, some of your accomplishments might be personal stories, rather than work situations. Use those to reveal aspects of your character—how you turned a 'C' into an 'A,' or overcame adversity, or learned about yourself and your workstyle through your hobbies. We recommend you generate an inventory of 8 to 12 solid accomplishments to highlight to specific audiences.

For each of your accomplishments, you may have obvious numerical results, such as "sales increased by $300,000 over the year." Most accomplishments, however, are not so well defined. Use the following checklist to develop concrete, quantified statements.

Reflect on the task purpose and the significance of completing the job. Somebody wanted something done and asked you to do it. What did that person want to get out of it?

Use percentages ("sales increased by 75%") or absolute values ("sales increased by $3 million dollars") to show your results in the best light.

You may emphasize what would have happened had you not been there: "If this had not been done successfully, the exhibition with 30,000 visitors per year could not have taken place."

The result might have helped improve results in another area: "By completing this task, the company was able to bid on million-dollar contracts that it otherwise would have been excluded from."

Results might be rescuing a bad situation: "Received a project that was over budget by 20%, and completed it on time and within original budget."

Avoid the use of "many" or "significant" and replace them with numbers: "across many time zones" becomes "across four time zones." "Several communities" becomes "12 communities."

Step 2: Learning through imitation

Imitation is the highest form of flattery, so in this step, we want you to review some example Accomplishments statements, covering a wide range of talents and experiences. Examine how these statements generally flow; use those expressions and structures you are most comfortable with in writing up your own statements.

By driving vision and strategy, creating a talented team, and building a customer service culture, grew a $75 million business into $680 million over a 12-year period. ***Results****: Produced year-on-year sales growth of 20% through product innovation and led the sale of the business to private equity investors.*

Passionate about driving improved business performance, volunteered to lead a high-risk project to salvage looming product and customer disaster, which involved recalling and reworking thousands of faulty high-profile products. ***Results****: Within six months: (i) successfully reworked and redeployed all products while rebuilding customer satisfaction; (ii) drove significant internal process improvements across multiple company functions,* *and (iii) project became template for new function with responsibility for all new product introduction (NPI) activities throughout the company.*

Designed and built a living room chair using steel and wood. Used alternative design details to overcome construction problems. Contrasted the properties through design, yet connected the two seamlessly. ***Results****: Received compliments from the head of the Architectural department, peers, and many others. Customers made offers to purchase the chair as well as suggestions to produce and present it to the market.*

Developed an eye for seeing what needs to be done and doing it. While a project manager at ABC Cloud Computing, became the go-to person for critical customer issues and software scalability considerations. ***Results****: Helped drive highest levels in customer responsiveness while leveraging customer insights to improve software architecture and scalability by a factor of 4 times.*

Completed the design and development of a medical instrument to analyze breath samples for detection of gastrointestinal disorders. When the original project was struggling, revised and adapted the project using newer components and software techniques to produce a smaller, cheaper, and more robust design. ***Results****: This design was crucial in producing a marketable instrument for a large multinational drug corporation with over $2 billion in sales annually.*

Developed a real-world simulator demonstrating the capabilities of fuzzy logic in solving complex tasks. This work required long hours of study and extensive research. ***Results****: Completed a thesis at University XYZ as part of the requirements for the masters of engineering degree and published a paper in the IEEE Transactions on Instrumentation and Measurement.*

Step 3: Giving your accomplishments weight

For each of your accomplishments, read the resulting paragraph a few times. The results should:

Elicit a sense of satisfaction and accomplishment;

Answer the question, "How does this make you different from others?"

If your paragraphs do not pass these tests immediately, keep tightening them until they pass.

Keep in mind why you are writing these statements—to show your personality. It is not about the task. The task details are only for credibility. When you say you are "determined" and show an example of this determination supported by facts, figures, names, and details, the personality work style takes on an unquestioned credence.

Stage 2: Creating an Impressive *Opportunity Sought*

Now that you feel confident about your previous accomplishments, it's time to turn to the future. This section must deliver a substantial, concise message about who you are, what you are looking for, and what results you can deliver. Think of it as the title of your résumé, and as such, it is the **most important section for the reader.** This section must:

Be clear (avoid vagueness) and brief

Gain the reader's attention

Describe the job function, not the job title

Describe industry sector (only if it is important to you)

When written well, an *Opportunity Sought* statement should allow the reader to visualize you in that role and see how you are functioning, without being artificially restrictive to an industry or organization.

Here are some *Opportunity Sought* statement examples:

To secure a managing or supervisory position in purchasing or inventory handling for a medium- or large-sized company in the aerospace industry.

To direct and operate a mid- to large-sized company or department involved in the development and distribution of IT goods or services, or other business sector. To be involved in the business planning and organizational development with the goal of improving operational and financial positions.

To run retail or other business operations or projects and use my experience as a process troubleshooter to improve business results. To establish and implement programs and procedures such as inventory control, taking advantage of my ability to switch gears in a moment's notice. With the above tasks, to follow through quickly with a no-nonsense approach and within cost budgets.

To develop, test, and troubleshoot computer-based information management systems, including business applications such as workflow and configuration management. To interface with clients, users, peers, and juniors in delivering those systems to improve organizational operations.

To oversee a technical development group or department with attendant quality assurance section, preferring the domain of medical software or hardware, or other software development and quality assurance domains. Seeking the challenge of improving the department's performance through precise, hands-on management derived from innovation, testing, feedback, and relationship building based on respect for the individual, the team, and superiors.

A part-time position as a senior advisor to the executive team members, where my broad management experience, engineering background, strong communication and negotiation skills, and corporate social responsibility practice can contribute to the venture's ongoing success.

Your career choice should be about loving your job, getting up in the morning excited (or even anxious) to go to work. Anything else would be a daily struggle. Thus, you must begin with a fresh sheet of paper, regardless of your experiences, as you design your work objective. Of course, you must be realistic. However, based on your skills and experience, you should describe in your Opportunity Sought why a position attracts you.

Step 1: Brainstorming your Opportunity Sought

When many people think about their next career move, they're not sure what they want to do. They desire change, but lack direction. This is common. Here's how to proceed:

Schedule a brainstorming session with a career coach or with a trusted, positive-minded confidant. Don't go through this exercise with a "Negative Nelly" who will continually remind you, "That's unrealistic," or says, "Set your sights lower!" During your brainstorming session, describe where you see yourself in five years:

Where are you?

Who are you with?

What are you doing?

What type of work are you doing?

Are you working for yourself? A Corporation? A nonprofit organization?

What type of service or product are you involved with?

Let your mind wander unrestrictedly and talk aloud as you describe your desirable situation and condition. Your coach/confidant will be listening; you should both write down words and thoughts. After 15 or 20 minutes, work with your coach/confidant to group those words and thoughts under as many headings as needed. Review your notes and regroup those headings into two or three categories. This exercise can help you figure out which careers interest you.

You may have more than one interest. If so, write up an Opportunity Sought statement for each. If you do create multiple

Opportunity Sought statements initially, think about how you might condense them into one statement. The more unique your Opportunity Statement is, the easier it is to stand out from the crowd.

Step 2: Developing and testing your Opportunity Sought statement

In your journal, capture some thoughts around the following questions:

What thrills you at work?

What do you struggle with at work?

State your preferred position objective (e.g., supervisory position), keeping it as flexible as you want.

Identify the company section or group if needed (e.g., the Purchasing department).

State your desired organization size and industry section (e.g., in a medium-sized aerospace company).

Describe where geographically you want to work, if relevant (e.g., in Canada, the United States, Latin America).

Now combine these thoughts into a few sentences, such as in the examples provided earlier, and think about your statement. Is it complete? Does it paint a clear picture of what you want to be doing? Is it compelling to the reader?

Use this test to reflect on your thoughts: *Does the role excite me?* Keep at it until you are sure.

Keep in mind the test that the employer uses:

Do I have such a position (or need) available?

Do I understand what she actually would do?

Do I value the special skills she claims to bring to this job?

Do I see that she understands the business?

Now I want to read more about her... let's see the rest of her résumé.

Step 3: Testing your Opportunity Sought (checklist)

We have sometimes found people struggle to achieve transparency in their personal Opportunity Sought; use this checklist as a final step to help you finalize your statement. This portion of your résumé is crucial, and if you don't get it "right," your résumé will appear unfocused and not capture the reader's attention. Ensure that you:

Explain to the reader in simple language what job you want. Clarity is essential if you want a busy person to pay attention to your résumé. The reader wants to make a decision quickly, which is in both parties' best interests. If it's not a good fit, you can both move on.

Avoid generalities and focus on specifics. Busy people want to know what you are talking about and understand your statement. If you describe a job the reader currently has available, you will resonate with him more than a vague applicant will.

Ensure the words are in the order of importance to you. For example, you might write, "A sales and marketing position," but if the priority is the reverse for you, then write, "A marketing and sales position."

Convey your passion to the reader. We know you are passionate about the role; share that excitement with the reader. That person wants excited employees, not disengaged workers (the unfortunate norm in most workplaces).

Read your statement and get excited at the prospect of landing such a job. If you're not excited about the opportunity, you are barking up the wrong tree. You need to rethink your statement and reconstruct a more commanding statement.

Follow an easy-to-read writing style. Be careful using technical industry terms—the first person who sees your résumé may not be the one who would employ you, may not understand the trade jargon, and could reject your résumé simply because he or she did not understand your technical language.

Keep your message simple. If you water down the soup, it never tastes as good. Every extra word you have competes with the main message therein. The fewer extraneous words, the more focus will shine on the remaining words you want to convey to the prospective employer.

Use the most important words or phrases first and least important last. The reader is trying to get through your résumé quickly so he or she can move on to the next résumé. You want the most important word to imprint upon that person's mind first to quickly communicate your message.

Use applicable specifics. In one of our examples, we stated, *"To oversee a technical development group or department with attendant quality assurance section, preferring the domain of medical software or hardware, or other software development and quality assurance domains".* The main message is *"To oversee a technical development group."* The applicable specifics are *"... with attendant quality assurance section, preferring the domain of medical software or hardware."*

Expand your options to broaden your chances. In the same example, we expand our options by adding, *"... or other software development and quality assurance domains,"* which aligns with the applicant's skill set.

Indicate your personal strengths (applicable to the position). Another example stated, *"To run retail or other business operations or projects and use my experience as a process troubleshooter to improve business results."* This adds personal strengths applicable to the position: *"To set up and implement programs and their procedures, such as inventory control, taking advantage of my ability to switch gears in a moment's notice. With the above tasks, to follow through quickly with a no-nonsense approach and within cost budgets."*

Note any restrictions. *"Seeking a locally-based company (preferably global in scope with up to 25% travel time."* Only include these potential restrictions if they are truly important to you.

Indicate what you hope to get out of the job. Another example stated, *"To interface with clients, users, peers, and juniors in delivering those systems."* This desire might speak to your collaborative nature (possibly an **F** work style) and should be included if relevant.

Indicate what you can bring to that position. The reader should visibly see how you would add value to the organization: *"...with the goal of improving its operational and financial position"*; *"...contribute to the success of a new or ongoing venture."* The more specifics you can provide on how you can help the organization, the more you will gain the reader's attention.

Indicate what you don't want. For example, you might want to be a sales team manager, but not want to handle a sales portfolio at the same time. Thus, if that is important to you, say so.

If you are new to the trade, make that known. Explain to the reader what, despite your newness, you bring to the position.

Here's the real test: When done, say to yourself, "Wow, I would feel terrific if I had that job." If you don't feel that way, go back to the drawing board. Your statement must pass that test, and only you can be the judge.

Stage 3: Describing Your Capabilities

The Capabilities section illustrates you can do what the reader needs and what you want to do. These two opening sections of your résumé should captivate the reader.

Here are some examples of how the Opportunity Sought statement and the Capabilities section fit together (the **bolded words** are key words, which you'll create shortly):

OPPORTUNITY SOUGHT:

To **teach** engineering-related topics **at a university or college** and apply my extensive industry-based **research experience** to organize, plan, and direct departmental operations in a scientific or **technical faculty**.

CAPABILITIES:

- Seven years teaching at the University of ABC and XYZ College
- Three years managing operations research programs for the military
- Credited with five electronic inventions
- 20 years planning environment for multibillion dollar telecommunications firm JKL
- 20 combined years of managing technical staff

OPPORTUNITY SOUGHT:

Recent architect graduate seeking a position in a design/build firm providing **customized designs**. A position within a development, architectural, or design firm where I can apply my design, construction, and **problem-solving skills** during **all phases of the project**, from conceptual ideas to overseeing its construction.

CAPABILITIES:

- B.A.S., Architectural Studies – XYZ University, 2014
- Proficient with AutoCAD, Form Z, and Photoshop
- Helped design and construct a 2,300 sq.' individualized family cottage
- Founded a successful design/renovations company and managed it for three summers
- Lecturer and problem-solver in Architectural Draughtsmanship, West Africa, 2015
- Redrafted 'as-builts' for a 250,000 sq.' light manufacturing building

OPPORTUNITY SOUGHT:

To work in an organization with local and **international clients** in a long-term relationship-building role in a coaching, training, or **business sales** capacity. To inform, train, enhance, coach, and motivate people to **improve their current work situations**, and to build those relationships over the long term. Seeking employment in a small- to medium-sized, professional, dynamic company with a proven track record.

CAPABILITIES:

- Advised people in 10 cities in United States and Canada with personal and business time-management issues
- Four years coaching and training hundreds of people to improve their businesses
- 10 years of business consulting with six U.S. Federal Government departments
- 14 years in sales, winning top sales and performance recognition four times
- Completed training courses in sales development, motivation, self-awareness, conflict resolution, and facilitation

In summary, your Capabilities **demonstrate and verify you have the qualifications to fulfill the role** of the Opportunity Sought. They must:

Be brief and easy to scan (preferably a bulleted list);

Support or reinforce every key word in Opportunity Sought, but no more than that so as to not water down your message;

List relevant experience, education, and training;

Answer the following: What does the employer want to see that shows that you can do the job? What will make the employer want to talk with you?

Show proof numerically in every instance above;

Describe your "approach" or method, but only if relevant; remember, the point of the *Capabilities* section is to emphasize the *Opportunity Sought* statement.

The Capabilities section reinforces a solid, consistent message. It should be direct and to the point. If written correctly, the reader will pay attention to your résumé, rather than just scan it. This is your ultimate goal: to get the reader reading your résumé right from the start.

Step 1: Building first cut Capabilities, then iterating

Go back through your *Opportunity Sought* statement word by word and:

Underline every **key word** (see earlier examples).

List a corresponding bulleted item in the same order as the key words appear in the statement. Include only experience, ability, times, numbers, etc.

Reread your statement to ensure you didn't miss anything and there is nothing extraneous in either section.

Iterate: As you develop this section, you may find yourself including other capabilities that are important to you, but not reflected in your *Opportunity Sought* statement. Therefore, insert the corresponding description into the Opportunity Sought. Make sure these blend without disrupting the flow or burdening the first part of the résumé.

Step 2: Testing your Capabilities section (checklist)

Examining your first cut of your Capabilities statements, check to confirm each statement:

Addresses each key word you underlined in the Opportunity Sought. If not, return to Opportunity Sought to question the word's relevance. This approach will ensure your consistency and conciseness.

Avoids adding irrelevant details to the Opportunity Sought. Just because you have a Ph. D., if it is not relevant, do not include it here. Show it in the **Education** section instead. Conversely, upon listing a previously missed special skill in Capabilities, return to the Opportunity Sought to check for a correlating reference. If you see the Ph. D. is relevant to this job, list it in Capabilities, but also go back to Opportunity Sought to add a reference to it in the appropriate place.

Associates a (quantifying) number with every bullet. Only numbers and names provide credibility. Add number of years, visitors, votes, companies, etc. Examples: "Reduced cost by 30% in one year," or "Spent six years in a manufacturing cost-reduction role with GE and HP."

Limits itself to no more than seven or eight bullets. No matter how good a four-hour movie is, the viewer's patience is taxed after two hours. Likewise, an eight-bullet Capabilities section is plenty for a busy reader. Remember not to water down your capabilities with less-important issues. If your Capabilities section is too long, your Opportunity Sought statement may also be too long.

Integrates fully with the Opportunity Sought statement. Note the iterative aspect to the development of these two sections. After one is completed, is the other one still in order?

Step 3: Sharing your work with a trusted confidant

As a final check of your Opportunity Sought and Capabilities, present them to a good friend or two and ask them if they:

Understand it.

Agree with it, inasmuch as they know you.

Can repeat it back to you (at least the highlights and main concept) without looking at it; if they can't, these both need more work.

Stage 4: Constructing Your Résumé

At this point, the hard work is over; the next sections are straightforward, and you already have most of the content you need. Page 2 of your résumé is the "been there, done that" page. You have already extracted the gems of your work and personal experiences in your **Accomplishments** section. Your future-oriented **Opportunity Sought** statement and supporting **Capabilities** paint a clear picture of what you want to be doing, and why you are capable of doing it masterfully. With all this in place, creating your page 2 content is easy.

Page 2 starts with a reverse chronological order listing of your employment history. You only need to include the company name, your most recent title, the years you worked there, and a brief description of either the company's focus or your focus while there. You only need the basics here because you already captured your significant results in your Accomplishments statement.

Step 1: Building page 2 of your résumé

Page 2 headlines the extensive experience you identified in your Capabilities section. Additionally, you will include other basic information, such as your education (if relevant) and possibly any pertinent hobbies, awards, and/or memberships.

This should be no longer than one page, which means whittling down the details and sticking with just the basics. Here are some ideas to get you started:

Start by listing out all your work experiences—one line per employer—and capture the start and end dates (years only is usually sufficient at this point);

If you have a few short stints, you can bundle them all together and present them collectively either as a period where you worked for "various companies" or possibly as a stint of self-employment, if that seems reasonably accurate (you are not trying to mislead, merely showing that you were gaining varied experiences to add to your "backpack");

If there is a significant gap in your work history, don't gloss over it; its absence will be obvious, and the reader will wonder what you did during that time. If you were travelling around the world, offer that up as a short explanation. If taking care of family members kept you from the traditional job market, tell the reader you were carrying out family obligations. A short explanation is always better than leaving a gap and letting readers decide for themselves what it means. Assuming you didn't just spend that whole year on the sofa watching TV, you most likely gained interesting experiences of some kind, and you want to address that briefly;

Similarly, you can show volunteer work without explicitly stating it as such. For example, if you worked with a local charity for the past few years a few evenings a week and helped them manage their retail operations, then you have applicable, valuable experience in retail operations. Being paid or not paid for that work is not germane as to whether you performed work assignments and did them well. Volunteer work can often provide strong Accomplishments statements; don't shy away from the experience you gained and your contributions just because it was an unpaid position.

Other information that you might want to highlight includes your educational levels, current board/association memberships, and possibly hobbies (if you have enough space and your hobbies are a source of pride and passion for you).

Avoid statements like "references available upon request" or other statements to that effect. They're unnecessary and waste valuable résumé space. When hiring managers are interested enough to contact you, they'll ask about references if that is a standard part of their process.

Step 2: Assembling your (second) résumé

We suggest you prepare two résumés. The first is a full résumé—your **master résumé**—which lists all 12 to 16 accomplishments and represents your complete "inventory." It also includes the second page, although by this point, your résumé may be three or four pages long, depending on the number of accomplishments in your inventory.

The second résumé, your **model résumé,** is the format you will actually send out to others. **It should be no longer than two pages** and only include your most relevant accomplishments. Sometimes your accomplishments may spill onto the second page; that's fine, as long as the total résumé does not exceed two pages. Now is a good time to "test" your résumé to ensure it captures all pertinent information in two pages. Once you are finished, your résumé will look like this:

Page 1:

Your name, centered, at the top of the page;

Your contact details (personal email and phone number), in the left/right margins at the top of the page;

Opportunity Sought: at the top of the page, in paragraph format, five to eight lines of written text;

Capabilities: listed below your Opportunity Statement, three to eight lines, bulleted list.

These should take up no more than one-third of your first page. The rest of the page lists the four to eight accomplishments that you are profiling in this version of your résumé. You will choose those selected accomplishments based on the opportunity and what the company is looking for. You are not rewriting your résumé for this opportunity; rather, you are "fine-tuning" it to best showcase you're an excellent fit (if the opportunity is not an excellent fit, you shouldn't be applying to it... we'll cover that in more detail in Section 3).

Page 2:

Again, the top line is your name and contact details;

Your work (and related) experience, listed in reverse chronological order, by name of organization;

For each separate organization (listing), a short description of the focus of your role, including job titles if relevant;

Educational history;

Board and association memberships;

Hobbies (again, if applicable to the story you are presenting about yourself).

Andrew Currie, one of Tim's coaching clients, followed this methodology and developed his résumé around his consulting offer of contract-based, executive team facilitation engagements. Again, note how this format captures the essence of an almost 30-year varied career comfortably within a two-page format. *(Company, client and institution names, and locations have been adjusted for privacy considerations; all other information contained is accurate.)*

ANDREW CURRIE

12345 Any Street
Your Town, State, Zip Code

(mobile): 888-555-1212
Andrew@emailaddress.com

Opportunity Sought:

I seek opportunities to "roll up my sleeves" and work closely with business owners/executives who are committed to driving their companies to higher levels of sustainable business performance. As a catalyst, I help management teams embrace new ways of looking holistically at their business, leading to dramatic improvements in the alignment of their business strategy with the operational aspects of their organizations. Passionate about business, I'm a lifelong student, teacher, and visionary actively exploring the theme of "business done well."

Capabilities:

- As principal of strategy business for 10+ years, engaged executive teams of 27 organizations to help them improve business strategies, simplify operations, and drive overall performance.
- 26 years of business experience working for 7 different companies in 8 executive roles, including CEO; extensive international experience, with 3 years in U.K.-based global mandate.
- As lifelong learner, have participated in over 50 technical, business, and executive development programs and courses to augment my foundation of engineering (BSc) and business (MBA) degrees.
- 8 years as university professor, emphasizing critical thinking in: (i) International Business, (ii) Marketing Strategy, (iii) Business Process Transformation (BPT), and (iv) Business and Society (Governance).

Selected Accomplishments:

Performed role of **catalyst** in driving executive-level conversation and process that led owner/founder of $2 billion global telecommunications company to recognize his company needed a dramatic, immediate restructuring. ***Results:*** Agreed restructuring plan led directly to successful company sale for $7.1 billion within 6 months.

Passionate about driving improved business performance, volunteered to lead high-risk project to salvage looming product and customer disaster. It involved recalling and reworking thousands of faulty high-profile products. ***Results:*** Over a six-month period: (i) successfully reworked and redeployed all products while rebuilding customer satisfaction; (ii) drove significant internal process improvements across multiple company functions, and (iii) project became template for new function with responsibility for all new product introduction activities throughout company.

In **Expert Advisor** roles for various funding organizations, have provided **structured, analytical** reviews on business plans covering opportunities and industries from "green tech" to "nanotech." Overall portfolio examined over 6 years includes 19 detailed funding proposals in green tech business initiatives, and more than 80 nanotech project proposals. ***Results:*** Subsequently engaged by each funding organization to help improve business processes in their respective organizations; each became more widely regarded as effective funding bodies in their specific industry circles.

Structured and implemented a cost-effective comprehensive market and competitive research process in a $300 million product business unit of a $15 billion global company. ***Results:*** (i) Framework served as foundation for most successful executive "war games" in business unit history. This led to refocusing of business, and, through internal "best practices" involvement of staff, ii) was assessed as most advanced process throughout the whole company; (ii) subsequently won the coveted President's Award.

Accountable for newly created role of Partner Marketing, worked with various sales and support functions to re-align European marketing and sales efforts to provide more consistent and comprehensive VAR, OEM, and Reseller support. ***Results:*** over a 15-month period, the region enjoyed a doubling of OEM revenue generation, an 80% growth in traditional channel sales, and a tripling in business sales of affiliated products.

Entrusted with a "flashing red critical priority" project in a $500M company, **envisioned** and restructured the technical communications and priority processes between Far East manufacturing centre and local design authority. ***Results:*** New processes implemented within four weeks. All critical and priority issues were resolved within six months. Technical support systems became company showcase processes and earned several executives significant promotions.

During the critical early days of a multibillion dollar acquisition integration, provided the **catalyst** for the existing eBusiness function to become the acquirer's Center of Excellence, responsible for all activities across their $30 billion global business platform. ***Results***: Delivered strong post-acquisition morale in the acquired company and retained employee engagement in a critical time, which allowed the acquirer to leverage their newly purchased assets effectively.

Professional Experience:

FOUNDER AND OWNER, Currie Strategy Consulting (CSC) **2003–Present**
Work with executive teams & business owners to maximize company success. We focus on executive facilitation leading to strategy alignment and action plan development to accelerate performance.

PROFESSOR, University Business School **2003–2010**
Part-time professor (Marketing, Business Process Redesign, CSR, International Business) in both undergraduate and graduate teaching levels.

PRESIDENT AND CEO, Video-Capture Inc. **2000–2002**
Mandated to transform seed-funded "science project" start-up and founding team into commercially viable high growth company with real market traction and capable of attracting appropriate institutional funding.

Assistant VP, DIRECTOR, Asynchronous Networks (Ottawa–4 years; UK–3 years) **1993–2000**
Contributed to company's growth from $180 million to $2 billion through major roles in revenue generation, alliance development, product & portfolio management, business development, and financial oversight. Directly involved in setting the stage for successful global acquisition of company.

MARKET SPECIALIST, Norrada Networks **1992–1993**
Developed market and customer intelligence infrastructure for $300 million business division; contribution recognized through winning of President's Award of Excellence.

DIRECTOR, Middletech Corporation **1985–1991**
Significant successes in supporting operations-driven turnaround of company through streamlining major business processes, reducing product variation, and improving product and process quality.

Previous Selected Work Experience **1980–1985**
Government of Canada contracts (software development); High-Energy Laser Lab (university research labs); Canaxia Gas Facilities (junior engineer); Synthesis Canada (junior engineer).

Education and Interests:

M.B.A., University of XYZ (1993)
B.Sc. Engineering, University of ABC (1983)
Hobbies include snowboarding, biking, hiking, and family road trips
Contributing writer to various publications; blogger at http://andrewcurrie.com

Stage 5: Creating Your Biography and Tagline

You've assembled your main story in your master résumé; now you will create two other essential items: your **biography** and a short **tagline**.

Step 1: Writing your biography

Your biography is a short summary for people who have an interest in you and want to know more:

Name: Start with a one-line heading of your usual name, bold and centered, 14-point font.

Position Title: Take the title of the position from Opportunity Sought (shorten if too long).

Business Sector: Indicate the business sectors in which you are interested and/or have experience.

Degree of Experience: Provide general number of years in the business and/or number of employees supervised.

Specific Experience: Give a short description of your work history. You may decide to combine the Degree of Experience with the Specific Experience if you prefer that format.

Education: Show degree or certification and institution.

Geography: Describe where you are and where you want to go.

Special Skills: Inject a word or two in the text illustrating any related special skills.

Now put it all together in less than 100 words. Here is an example:

John Smith

Operations director in recreation, hospitality, and other customer service-driven industries. Over 15 years of business experience in public and private sectors. Stabilized business with staff of 150 and made it profitable by introducing best practices and holding staff and suppliers accountable. Managed capital improvements exceeding $4 million on time and on budget. Law degree in French at Université de ABC, Master of Business Administration courses at the University of XYZ. Presently located in Springfield, Ohio, and willing to relocate anywhere in eastern North America, preferably in a bilingual environment.

Step 2: Writing your personal tagline

When you meet someone new, you must be able to articulate who you are to that person, and you need to do it quickly. This is your tagline, often referred to as your "elevator pitch." The basic rule with the tagline is **the shorter and catchier, the better.** It serves to act as a hook and intrigue the listener. Brief guidelines are as follows:

Use your biography as a starting point. Stick to three points (most people won't remember more than that).

Make all three points memorable so the listener will remember something special about you.

Adapt at least one of your points to the situation to show relevance.

If you are changing careers, add one more sentence indicating where you are going.

Look back at John Smith's biography again. John might come up with this three-point tagline:

Starting with a French law degree in and an MBA, I have been an operations director in the customer service industry for 15 years. I lead an organization of 150 people that specializes in turnarounds of unprofitable business units.

Now comparing that tagline against the criteria above:

Stick to three points:

Education: law degree and MBA

Experience: 15 years in customer service

Scope: 150-person staff, focus on profits

Make the three points memorable:

Education: two degrees, one in French

Experience: 15 years

Scope: 150 staff, focus on profits that trigger a "wow"

Adapt the three points to the situation:

If you are talking to someone from the hospitality industry, then adapt your experience to specifically call out your background in the hospitality industry:

"...My past 15 years were spent as operations director in hospitality and customer service industries."

If you are seeking an entirely new trade or profession, add a sentence about the new direction

Stage 6: Using LinkedIn and Social Media

Your résumé is a great starting point, but in our online and highly connected world, it isn't enough anymore. Most of the organizations to which you apply will check you out online, and many base their decisions on what they find. If you are looking for work in any capacity, your online presence is crucial. Be proactive. Manage the information people will see about you.

LinkedIn, the world's most popular professional network, is one of the best resources to help you manage your online reputation, since profiles tend to show up highly in search engine results and is one of the favorite locations for prospective employers to search for candidates.

Here is why you need to develop a great LinkedIn profile:

Prospective employers are going to Google you, and LinkedIn is one of the easiest ways to show up highly on a search result.

LinkedIn is the best place for professional visibility.

Many companies use LinkedIn to post jobs, and the site's tools are helpful for anyone involved in a career search.

Demonstrating online skills in today's internet-dependent world is particularly important to many prospective employers, and having an online presence is crucial.

LinkedIn is an excellent place to build a professional network. In order for people to want to connect, you must make sure that your profile is professional, accurate, and current.

LinkedIn and how viewers "see you"

Before we dive into how to build an enthralling LinkedIn profile, let's look first at how a potential employer reviews someone's profile. A 2012 study of an eye-tracking heat map (software that tracks where people look when scanning a webpage) showed that recruiters spent 19% of their total time reviewing profile pictures; then, they glance at the current job position and education sections, followed by skills, specialties, and/or work experience. While LinkedIn continues to evolve and is often changing the structure of how public profiles flow, the main takeaways from this survey are:

Our eye first goes to the visual (picture), so make sure you have a professional, engaging picture of yourself on your profile that complements your overall storyline;

Your headline is right next to your picture, and most viewers are spending some of that 19% "picture time" scanning your headline to get a sense of what you do;

Viewers then scan down through the summary, and if still interested, move on to work experience. If you can't hook them in those first few seconds, they will lose interest and move on to another profile.

Components of your LinkedIn profile

Much like your résumé, your LinkedIn profile has numerous sections; the most important are Name, Photo, Headline, and Summary. A comprehensive review of these fields, along with guidance on how to complete each one, follows.

Section	Guidance
Name	Your name (how you want people to refer to you). Avoid cute nicknames.
Photo	A good photo helps you connect with people (they see your face). Be genuine; make sure your photo is current and professional. Smiles are preferable.
Headline (Title)	A description of yourself in 120 characters or less. After your photo and name, your headline is the next most viewed part of your profile. Make it count. Focus on the value you provide. What makes you stand out? This is your opportunity to catch readers' attention so they want to read more. Include keywords that might be used in searches (e.g., if you are a product manager, make sure to include 'product manager' in your title). Provide a condensed overview of who you are, your personal story, and your value proposition. Use your most descriptive keywords to highlight the authentic you.
Summary	This section is crucial—it's the 'go-to' portion of your profile, the main section people will read to learn about you. Most people take about 30 seconds to review a profile online, longer if they see something of interest. Since this is the make-or-break part of your profile, compiling your Summary may be difficult. This easy-to-read narrative should only be two to four short paragraphs. This is not a rehash of your experience, but a brief snapshot of your worth to captivate your reader's interest.
Experience	A chronological listing of places you have worked. Just as you did when creating your résumé (assuming you used a chronological format), write in a more 'accomplishments-oriented' fashion, not just listing the job responsibilities. Make sure to communicate your achievements accurately without overwhelming the reader with too much description. résumé
Additional Information / Interests	This section helps potential employers and others connect with the interesting and complex person that you are.
Honors & Awards	List any honors or awards you have received that show how you stand out. Make sure these are consistent with your overall message.
Organizations	Reference any relevant and volunteer organizations in which you have participated. This demonstrates to a prospective employer you are a contributor and get involved beyond just the things around you.
Recommendations	Well-written recommendations can be helpful, external validation points of your abilities, particularly if the people recommending you have strong profiles themselves. Creating a long list of recommendations is not the point; remember, readers have a limited attention span. Focus on a few recommendations that come from respected people.
Skills & Endorsements	This section can be useful to display and get validation from others that you have skills in various areas. Having said that, there are a variety of opinions about how important / useful these really are (since LinkedIn makes it a little too easy just to get people to endorse skills sets even when they may know very little or nothing about you).

Section	Guidance
Education	List of educational establishments, what degree(s) or program(s) you completed, and when. Feel free to provide additional comments to highlight a specialization, achievement, or any other relevant point for each educational establishment. Although there is a section for Honors & Awards, you do not need to include those here, but may certainly reiterate them if you choose. Some redundancy can be useful, because you never know if someone quickly skimming your LinkedIn profile will see it the first time, and if it is a significant enough educational achievement, it is certainly acceptable and probably advisable to include it within the Education section.
Connections	LinkedIn is an excellent way to connect with other professionals. A profile with very few connections tends to communicate to others that you are a new user, an inactive user, and/or not very well connected. Work to acquire at least 200 connections. Having said that, the quality of your connections is also important, so make sure you grow your network with people that you would want others to see as 'in your network.' Your connections communicate a great deal about your brand, so make sure they are consistent with the image you want to project. Ideally, you want to work your way up to the 500+ number of connections (the top-advertised level on LinkedIn).
Groups	Similar to Connections, your association with other people, the clubs, communities, groups, etc. you join sends a message to others, which contributes to their perception of you. What groups could you join, and contribute to, that would help your online reputation? You can join numerous groups that will provide excellent content, discussions, and opportunities to contribute to the communities in which you are interested and that support your brand. Consider each group carefully to make sure that what it communicates about you is consistent with your areas of interest. While it's fine to join LinkedIn groups that do not align with your career interests (prospective employers like to see that candidates have varied interests), be careful to avoid the impression that you lack focus. For example, if you join 20 different LinkedIn groups that cover 10 different areas, people might perceive you as unfocused, and as a result, get a negative impression of you. Remember that people are mostly learning about you solely through your profile. The point of an online professional presence is to manage the perceptions of others, so make sure you consider the impact of what you put in your profile and how others may view you.
Following	Again, like Connections and Groups, who you follow sends a message and influences your online reputation. While the chance of people scrutinizing your followers is unlikely, make sure that you don't provide any red flags. People often see things in profiles (whether that be LinkedIn, Facebook, or other social media site) that turn them off from a candidate. In fact, for people who are not careful about managing their online reputation, it is more likely that someone will find a turn-off than a turn-on. Bottom line: consider each item in your profile and make sure it reinforces what you want others to see and think about you.

People often see things in profiles (whether that be LinkedIn, Facebook, or other social media site) that turn them off from a candidate. In fact, for people who aren't careful about managing their online reputation, it's more likely that someone will find a turn-off than a turn-on. Bottom line: consider each item in your profile and make sure it reinforces what you want others to see and think about you.

Advanced LinkedIn options

LinkedIn allows you to consider going above and beyond to differentiate yourself even further from others. The following more advanced options might be worth considering, depending on your circumstances:

Add more photos or videos. While this is obvious for some professions, such as artists or reporters, it can help anyone. Consider adding a video (about one minute long) to your profile. Focus on value-added professional content. Including additional photos and videos will help you stand out and be noticed (and remembered).

Add more sections to your profile. If you know multiple languages, add a section called "Languages." If you have published content, include a section called "Publications." If you have any patents, you can add a section called "Patents."

Final tips

Here are a few miscellaneous tips:

Take advantage of LinkedIn's help feature.

Visit the LinkedIn forum, which provides an interactive discussion and assistance on profile creation.

Make sure your profile is public (assuming you want people to see you in searches), though you may want to keep your profile private while you are still creating your initial profile as a new user.

Include your LinkedIn URL in your email signature: it's a good indicator you are trying to increase your professional presence.

Don't make your profile a replication of your résumé. Leverage LinkedIn for what it is: a professional networking tool. You can do a lot on LinkedIn to spark people's attention. Your résumé is brief;

LinkedIn is your opportunity to provide an enriched version of you.

As with any professional communication, make sure everything in your profile shouts excellence. Nothing spells low quality more than typos and grammatical errors. If you are not a good proofreader, get someone else (or several others) to review your profile and point out any errors.

Update your profile regularly. The more active you are, the more frequently you will show up in searches. Prospective employers view active LinkedIn users as more promising candidates.

The best advice we can give is to make sure you know your first-level connections. With whom we affiliate speaks volumes about who we are. When we connect with people we don't know, we risk connecting with people who are better not to be associated with. Additionally, we communicate a connection to others that doesn't truly exist, which can be embarrassing if someone asks you to connect someone to a first-level connection on your list and you're forced to admit you don't know that person.

Step 1: Mapping your biography and tagline onto your LinkedIn profile

Having condensed your story for your résumé, you now have the luxury of unlimited space to add supporting details that further enhance your story and amplify your overall message. This is not the time to lose your discipline by including unrelated information. Instead, let's map your work already completed into LinkedIn:

Headline = your tagline: Your written tagline probably runs to 30 to 50 words and clocks in about 12 to 15 seconds of speaking. You now need to reduce that to about 120 characters. Take the main ideas from your current tagline and reduce again. For example, the John Smith example earlier might have a LinkedIn headline such as, **"Richly experienced in the operations of customer service industries, I focus on turnarounds to profitability."** Don't be afraid to experiment with your own headline; it may well take several revisions before you are satisfied. Also, don't waste this valuable real estate on words like "currently unemployed" or "seeking opportunity." You can disclose that information in other sections.

Summary: Here again, you can repurpose your story elements as your starting point. The Summary builds from the **biography** and your **Headline.** A simple approach is to break the Summary into parts: (1) who you are; (2) your background and experience; (3) your prominent successes or accomplishments, and (4) what you seek. You can also mix in parts of your **Opportunity Sought** statement and **Capabilities** section to complete your Summary. While the Summary has no maximum length, keep in mind that people tend to scan LinkedIn profiles, just as they do with résumés.

Experience: Highlights the **work experience statements** from page 2 of your résumé. You can now build up each experience to showcase more of the "how you get things done." For each organization you include, go back through your **Accomplishments** and add them back into the relevant section of your Experience section on LinkedIn. As a first step, you can cut and paste them directly into LinkedIn. Once you complete your profile, reread it carefully and make sure it flows naturally.

Since most viewers spend the majority of their time viewing these sections of your profile, make sure they are solid and present a riveting story before moving on to the other components of LinkedIn.

By focusing your efforts and tightening those sections, you present an attractive, realistic view of yourself, and your profile has the chance to stand out from others.

Now we'll explore the final aspect of how to package and present your **compelling value story** through other social media avenues.

Using other social media effectively

Social media is no longer optional for people serious about their jobs and careers. If you are mid- or late-career and have eschewed it until now, it's time to create an effective online strategy. If you are early in your career, you have grown up with it and the risks are different. There will be a transition from using it with college friends and other twentysomethings (where talking about Spring Break indiscretions is expected), to managing your profile so that employers won't run in the other direction.

Think of yourself as the "brand champion" for the "product" that is you: the brand that you want to promote is your compelling value story. What you want to do first is understand your current online brand (or reputation). Is it attractive? Does it align with your story? Is it all you want it to be?

A word of caution here: social media can absorb a massive amount of time, so be very clear as to what you are trying to achieve in your social media strategy; we help you figure that out in Step 3.

Step 2: Researching your current online reputation

To know how others perceive you in the online world, you need to do a little investigative research of your online presence.

1. Google yourself. Type in your name and city and scan through the twenty pages of the search results (most people never click through to the second page of a search engine, so while the first page of your personal search is most important, you want to do your due diligence).

2. Take notes. Ask yourself: What would potential employers or collaborators think if they saw my current online presence?

3. Think about what you want your reputation to be. What do you want to be known for (your branding objective)? This should align with your personal brand, and will flow naturally from the work you have done so far in this book.

4. List one or more **branding objectives** to build into your ongoing social media activities. Keep the list brief; for example, *"To be perceived as an authority in software project management trends."*

Step 3: Cobbling together your social media strategy

Now that you have a sense of your current online reputation and visibility, you have to decide what you are prepared to do—and how much time you can invest—with the different social media tools available. Before jumping straight into any social media activity, it's important to create a general strategy, which you'll start to develop now.

For each of your **branding objective statements,** expand them now to include specifics about the intended audience, frequency, etc.

For example, our earlier "project management trends authority" objective can be more fully developed by our intended audience, communication frequency, and technical focus.

> *"To be perceived as an authority in software project management, specializing in exploration of emerging development methodologies and their most effective uses. To create a weekly communication of 10 minutes or less that contains quick tips for project managers (practitioners) and strategic content for decision-makers."*

Now that you have more clarity on what you are trying to accomplish within your branding objectives, **determine how much time you can and will commit** to building your online audience and reputation. Following our example, you might think through this as:

> *Software project management trends fascinate me, and I am researching new trends through various newsletters, magazines, and technical papers.*
>
> *I spend about five or six hours per week reading material, and if I could commit another two hours per week sharing my knowledge through social media, I could build an audience and my own credibility over time.*

Now that you have an idea of how much time you are willing to put into your social media branding objective, you must figure out which activities will help you achieve that objective. This will be a combination of answers to multiple questions:

> **What social media platforms does your intended audience currently frequent, and how do they like to consume relevant information?** Use LinkedIn, Facebook, and Twitter as your starting points. To find out what other channels are available, you could query project managers and decision-makers you know (or meet through networking activities, as we'll discuss in the next section) about what social media tools they use professionally.
>
> **What is the most effective way (for you) to communicate your message?** Some people are prolific writers, and so for them, blogging might be ideal; others communicate better verbally (podcasts) or through video (YouTube channels). Alternately, some social media tools feature slide sharing (PowerPoint presentations), photos, eBooks, surveys, polls, and an ever-

growing set of new platforms. Communicate your message in a way that comes naturally to you.

Does your communication preference match your intended audience's content preference? If there is a mismatch between your communication platform and how your audience likes to receive information, your message won't be heard.

What if my preference doesn't match my audience's preference? First, determine if you are comfortable with adapting your communication method, since your whole objective is to build credibility with a specific audience. If you don't think you can do that, then explore if you can compromise your preferred approach with your audience's preference. For example, write blog posts, and then record them and post them as podcasts. You could also write a blog post and have a friend interview you (in podcast format) about the post and its content. This way, you've created two different content pieces that complement each other and promote your growing authority in the field.

The next few pages list popular social media channels (most of which are generally free and easy to set up). Quickly scan through them now and think about which might work well with your communication style and resonate with your audience.

Start experimenting with your chosen social media tools. Don't over-think things at this point. You will discover what's working for you and what isn't, and the only way to truly learn this is by actually jumping in and getting started.

Finally, remember to **publish any social media sites where you have featured content.** Make sure the sites you list are up to date. It's never a good thing if you refer someone to a site where you haven't posted anything in a while. Encourage people to interact within your sites, and when they do, make sure you respond. This is one of the challenges of social media: limiting how much you do, since maintaining and responding to people can be time consuming.

Step 4: Picking through the cluttered social media landscape

The next few pages describe several sites that may help you improve your online reputation and achieve your branding objectives. When you do decide to further investigate any particular social media outlet, look online for a quick instructional video or article for some do's/don'ts and basic platform etiquette so you can decide if it is right for you.

Facebook: Facebook is a highly popular social media platform. While you can use it for professional purposes, it's been traditionally branded as a personal social media location. If you have a business or are an entrepreneur, Facebook can be a great place to promote your business because of its popularity and cost-effective, targeted advertising options. A word of caution: Make sure your profile portrays a positive, professional image. Prospective employers often search people's Facebook profiles, only to find embarrassing or unprofessional photos, comments, and images. Make sure all of your posts reinforce a consistent, professional, and positive story of you.

Google+: Having an active Google+ account can help with your Google search results. While Facebook is very popular, people tend to use it for personal purposes. Google+ users tend to project a more professional and organized approach to social media. LinkedIn should definitely still be your primary 'go-to' location for connecting with people; nevertheless, you can reach many people who aren't on LinkedIn through Google+. Maintaining and periodically updating your profile will increase the incidences of coming up in Google search results. This provides you with another way to influence the people who are looking for you, since you have control over your Google+ profile site.

YouTube: YouTube is the #1 video-sharing site, and the #2 most-searched engine on the planet (second only to Google, which also owns YouTube). If you want to increase your visibility, then YouTube is an excellent platform. Videos are becoming the preferred communication method these days. Make sure any videos you upload have high-quality video content, since a poor video will only harm your brand. YouTube lets you create your own 'channel,' a named location where you will post your content. Your channel lets you choose a distinctive URL where you can reference all your videos. Make sure the name reinforces your brand; a common choice is to use your name as your channel.

SlideShare (www.slideshare.net): If you have expertise in an area and excel at creating presentations, consider posting an original presentation on SlideShare. Each presentation you post receives a custom URL, which you can share with other people through your LinkedIn or Google+ profiles, in a tweet or an email, etc. SlideShare is an excellent way to display your creativity and ideas. Only post original presentations, and ensure that all of the content, including images, are legal for you to include. There are great stock photography sites, such as Shutterstock, where you can purchase right-to-use licenses for photos and illustrations at reasonable prices.

Twitter: Twitter can be an excellent place to get exposure. In a nutshell, Twitter is a personal broadcasting platform, enabling conversations between people with shared interests. You can also follow others and have others follow you. Since personal branding is about building your reputation, Twitter can be a great resource when used effectively.

Visual communities (Pinterest, Instagram): When deciding if you want to use a visual community site, such as Pinterest or Instagram, ask yourself if there are creative, high-impact ways the site can reinforce your brand, build your reputation, and communicate your worth. Similar to Facebook and Twitter, you can follow and "like" people, and even start a dialogue with other users by posting a comment attached to a picture you like. Visual communities are ideally suited to people who are interested in media, communications, photography, fashion, or food industries, where the visual element is a huge component of the job. In addition, these communities are excellent avenues to generate a positive reputation and to back up your expertise in an area.

Blogging (Wordpress, Tumblr, Blogger): If you are an author, a reporter, a specialist in a subject, or just love to write, one of the best ways to showcase your work is through a blog. There are many free, popular, and well-read sites to set up your blog such as Wordpress.com, Tumblr, and Blogger. We recommend you create a blogging schedule and stick to it—your readers will come to expect it. By choosing regular intervals to post to your blog, you are also building a habit. A key point about blogging is the need for constancy. If you have a message, are a decent writer, and can be consistent, you likely have what it takes to blog. Verify that your blog reinforces your brand, and always consider new ways to increase its exposure.

Podcast: A podcast is typically in audio format, but can also be other formats (video, PDF, etc.) that can be downloaded to a computer or mobile device. There are also streamed podcasts, where the user must be connected to the internet while listening. Consider podcasting if you have an idea for an interesting series and are more comfortable with audio than written communications. The emphasis here has to be on a topic people will find interesting. Your podcast content will depend entirely on what you are trying to communicate about your brand. Conducting interviews work particularly well in podcasts. Make sure to get permission from everyone you interview to publish the podcast. As always, when creating content as part of a professional profile, make sure your content is high quality. What you post online speaks volumes about the authentic you, and possibly the only thing some people will see (or, in this case, hear) to help them decide if you are worth further attention. Main podcasting platforms include iTunes, blogtalkradio.com, digitalpodcast.com, and ipodder.org. There are also several reference sites online to help you learn about the mechanics of podcasting.

EBook publishing (Kindle): If your writing endeavors stretch beyond blogging and you have an idea for a book, consider the following reasons why writing an eBook may be a great addition to your professional profile:

It establishes you as an expert. Writing an eBook provides you with a platform to communicate your experience in a given subject. This will increase your credibility in your audience's eyes, causing them to consider contacting you if they need help in your area of expertise.

It increases interest in you. Publishing an eBook adds an interesting dimension to you. You will create an aura of authority about your chosen subject, and when looking to make connections and build relationships, being interesting is a huge plus.

You can feel better about yourself and your career prospects. When we have a piece of work that we can point to as our own, we are more likely to feel better about our accomplishments. This improved sense of confidence will show when interacting with others. While you may be able to create a residual income source with eBooks as part of a professional profile, the focus is more on writing the eBook. You may want to share your eBook for free to increase the likelihood people will read it, learn more about you, and become interested in talking to you.

Step 5: Considering other essentials

To differentiate yourself even further, you may want to consider additional branding elements. Many people leverage the power of their brand successfully, and as time goes on, we expect more and more people to expand their brand presence. What this means is simple: you will very likely need to familiarize yourself with additional branding elements and select one or more to add to your portfolio.

The list in this section is not meant to be comprehensive, though it does highlight some of the most important areas to consider. We are not suggesting you should add all of these elements to your professional profile. Be judicious; some of these are easy to navigate, while others require an ongoing commitment. These elements include:

Email signature blocks: This is an easy way to promote your brand messaging in your everyday email activities. Outlook (and most other email platforms) lets you create your own signature that is automatically included in every email you send. This signature can contain your tagline, contact details, website URLs, links to your social media platforms, company logos, Skype contact address, etc. Try not to go overboard with your contact information. Experiment with different signature blocks and the messaging (your tagline, for example) they contain, and ask friends and colleagues for feedback.

Business cards: A business card is an excellent way to communicate your brand. Consider a scenario where you are speaking to someone at an event or impromptu meeting, and you realize that this is the perfect time to get his or her card so you can follow up and invite him or her to connect with you on LinkedIn. The best way to ask people for their business card is first to hand them yours. When selecting a business card provider, do your research and make sure to get a professional-looking card. For a small extra cost, you can use both sides of the card for your message.

Video résumés: Video résumés are gaining popularity because they allow you to express your brand in an easily digestible format. According to career publisher Vault Inc., 89% of employers revealed they would watch a video résumé. This format allows them to assess the candidate's professional presentation and demeanor. Just like with LinkedIn (and all online communications), if you are going to create and share a video résumé, make sure it is outstanding. A poorly produced video résumé is worse than no video résumé at all. If you decide to create a video résumé, invest your time and energy in ensuring you end up with a short (one to two minutes), engaging, professional-looking product that will garner the positive attention you want.

Personal websites: Many platforms allow you to create a personal website quickly and easily. These days, the challenge is no longer technical; it is primarily about **design** and **content**. Most of the popular website creation tools help you with design by providing a selection of predesigned, attractive templates. You can typically customize the design by including your own pictures. If you are a contractor or entrepreneur, having an attractive and easy-to-navigate site is expected. However, spending a lot of time or money on fancy designs is usually a poor investment. To get your best return, focus on your content. Crafting your best story should be your biggest priority. You can choose either a 'canned' site or your own website that is more flexible, but requires more work to create and maintain.

Canned website: Several providers allow you to create a single or multipage website, including:

> **About.Me:** A very popular choice for building a simple and beautiful one-page site, this user-friendly site lets you set up your own custom URL.
>
> **Strikingly:** Lets you quickly and easily create your own site and choose a custom URL.
>
> **Google Sites:** Google Sites is an easy-to-use website creation service. Just as with Google+, Google will provide preference to information found within Google Sites for search engine results.

Custom website: While there are many options to consider when creating a fully personalized website, we recommend Wordpress, a free content management system for creating your own personalized website. We like Wordpress because it is popular, convenient, and flexible; additionally, there are independent Wordpress developers who can build you a high-quality website for a small cost.

SECTION TWO: Recap

This section helped you build the individual elements of your compelling value story and then package them into a strong, concise résumé. You took those elements into the online world of LinkedIn and then explored the rapidly expanding universe of social media. You developed your own personalized social media strategy based on your online objectives and preferences.

We made the point that your résumé is a vehicle for your brand, and your unique plotline is largely based on your **PAVF work style.** We also walked you through an analysis of how people actually read through a résumé;

We laid out the critical components of our two-page résumé format: the **Opportunity Sought** statement and **Capabilities** section, followed by selected **Accomplishments,** all on the first page. We referred to page 2 as your **"been there, done that"** page;

You refined your **Accomplishments** from Section 1 into strong statements by writing them around a specific **Key Descriptor** and communicating an effective **Results** statement;

You constructed a powerful **Opportunity Sought** statement and the supporting **Capabilities.** You worked through detailed checklists to tighten and strengthen these critical components;

You pulled it all together into your **master résumé** by combining these elements and building your own page 2 material. You completed your story elements by developing your **biography** and **tagline;**

Next, you jumped into **LinkedIn** and expanded your résumé to fit into LinkedIn's **Headline, Summary,** and **Experiences** structure;

As preparation for leveraging social media, you researched your current online reputation and developed specific branding objectives.

You took a quick tour of some current social media tools and thought about **your communication preferences**, **your audience's communication preference,** and **your potential time investment.** You also learned about other ways to share your story, including individualized websites, video résumés, email signature blocks, and business cards.

You've covered a lot of ground here, and have a well-crafted, persuasive story to share through your work thus far. The next section focuses on the networking discipline you need to develop to propagate your story while growing your network to find great opportunities.

SECTION THREE:
THE OUTSIDE JOB –
MODERN NETWORKING AND JOB-HUNTING SKILLS

The "inside job," as we have described it, is building self-awareness to create an optimal fit between your passion, your skills, and earning a living. Section 3 now tackles "the outside job": how you get the excellent work you have done in Section 2 out there, in the hands of decision-makers.

Most people go about the "outside job" in completely the wrong way. In this section, we are going to explain in four stages what you are doing wrong in your job hunts and how to fix it.

In **Stage 1,** we talk about how the job market really works, and what that means for your networking. In **Stage 2,** we introduce the science of networks and human connections and how that helps your job hunt. In **Stage 3,** we show how your job hunt resembles a salesperson's funnel, and give you some tools for managing your own job pipeline. Finally, in **Stage 4,** we share vital tips for closing the deal, including interviewing and package negotiations.

Stage 1: How the Job Market Actually Works

From the outside, the job market looks like a formal HR process similar to the diagram below. This is how most people think things work, and so they act accordingly:

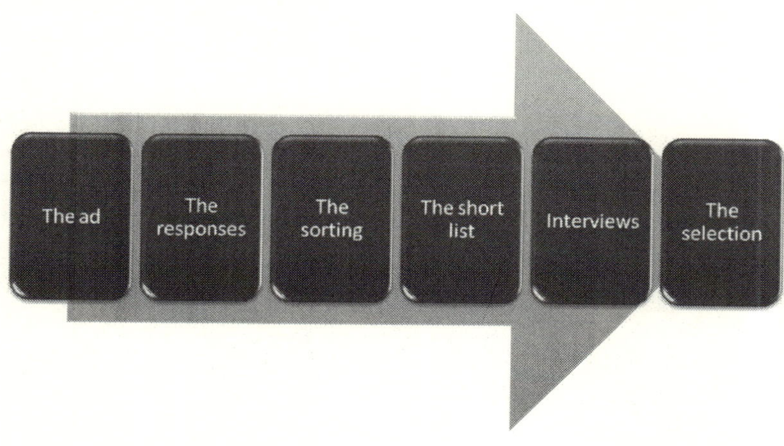

In this case, the best strategy is to apply for as many jobs as possible to increase our chances of securing an interview and ultimately landing a position. Typically, tailoring a résumé and cover letter to match the position takes one to two hours, including researching the job and the company. During that time, we become emotionally attached to the job from writing and rewriting our story. Our confidence in getting selected for the next step increases as we polish the application package. A dedicated job searcher might apply to three or five positions daily, and perhaps 15 to 20 in a given week, which can be time consuming and exhausting.

The problem is that the average posted job application in North America attracts hundreds of applicants. The person sorting through the résumés is usually not the hiring manager, but a junior staffer with limited time to select potential candidates. They play a "matching game." If the words in our résumé and cover letter match the words in the job description, we may get through. This is especially true when "bots" (automated screening software) are used. Invariably, a lot of arbitrary selection criteria work their way into the sorting process, as the sorter can only spend a minute or two on each résumé, which results in many perfectly qualified candidates never getting selected for the next step.

The probability of this method succeeding will depend on many things: the industry, economic climate, and how suited you are to the position. However, if the job is publicly posted, there may be hundreds of applicants, and we estimate the average success rate of this method is quite poor, perhaps as low as 300-to-1 for untargeted (shotgun) approaches.

Despite those long odds, most job seekers spend about 80% of their time in the cycle described above. The remaining 20% is spent at networking activities, job fairs, and similar activities. Yet the application cycle is grueling, and lack of success in online application can kill enthusiasm for the networking phase, revealing itself in a lackluster presentation style. Facing such circumstances, the typical job seeker withdraws more and more. This is much more so when the job seeker is unemployed or underemployed. This cycle of frustration, isolation, and withdrawal can be hard to break.

The consequences of this are huge:

The balance between 80% application and 20% networking must be reversed.

If "in transition" (unemployed), job seekers need to spend at least half their time "suiting up and showing up" (that is, meeting people) for two reasons. First, it counteracts the isolation that people feel when deprived of a work community. Second, valuable connections can be made.

Job seekers (or job changers) need to target employers and opportunities better and waste less time on shotgun approaches.

We base our main recommendation, the switch to 80% networking from 80% applying for jobs, because the **real** job market works nothing like the diagram above. There is a hidden, behind-the-scenes, process that the traditional application process ignores.

The Hidden Job Market and How It Works

Most organizations have a hidden process that happens before a formal job is posted either internally or externally that looks like this:

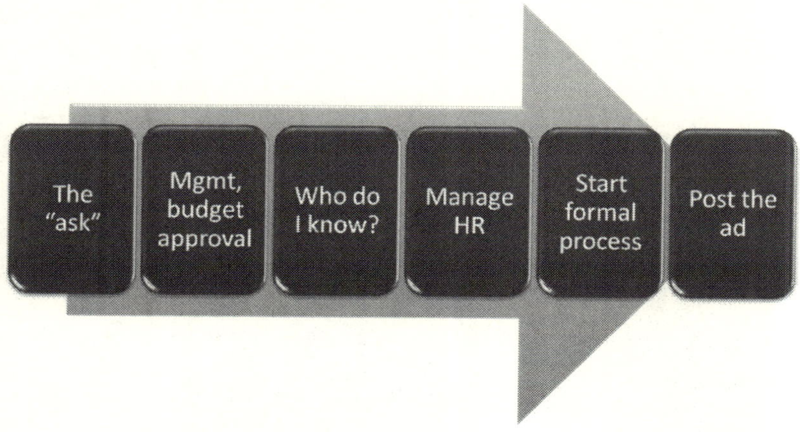

In this process, hiring managers think, "Who do I know that could do this?" As seasoned professionals, they probably know dozens of people at the level they are hiring, and possibly know one or two exceptional candidates. If not, while waiting for HR and budget approval, they might ask colleagues if they know of any qualified candidates. In the normal course of events, they will start putting out feelers, and may start the interviewing process even before HR approves the hire or advertises the job.

One of our clients related a story we have heard often. He was teaching part-time at a major university when the position for an associate dean of the business school opened up. He knew many faculty members who told him of the position, advised him to apply, and put in a good word with senior leadership. He swiftly interviewed with his eventual boss, several key faculty members, and within a week was informally offered the position. At the same time, a long, formal process was launched for the sake of appearances. The job was advertised, dozens of people applied, but the position had already been unofficially filled! This formal process is ostensibly to promote fairness and prevent nepotism, but several dozen people had their hopes lifted, and their time wasted, by a sham process.

Again, hard statistics are hard to come by, but we estimate that this informal process (through connections) is what really happens in **well over half the vacancies filled!** Dozens of hiring managers and job seekers have confirmed the outlined process above. Almost everyone has an example from their own experience that supports the premise most roles already have a preferred candidate earmarked, and the organization is often going through the motions more as a formality than for ensuring a truly objective, nonbiased selection process.

If you are applying to jobs through the formal process without any company connections, you are almost always in a similar situation. There are already a few preferred candidates, and a sea of applicants who essentially have little or no chance.

In our estimation, there is a 300-to-1 chance of landing a job through posting a résumé on an online job board, a 30-to-1 chance for formal applications for posted positions, and a 3-to-1 chance for preferred candidates.

So, how do you become a preferred candidate?

To become the preferred candidate in any job opening—formally posted or not—your best strategy is to continually and proactively grow your network so that you become part of other people's "trusted network." Then **you** become the person who has the inside track.

The problem is many people avoid networking, or do it incorrectly, for a few reasons:

They see networking as optional. We see it as essential! Even if you are blissfully happy in your role, more and more people are spending 5 years or less in their current jobs.

They have difficulty making the time to network. Time management is essential to business success. This means you must get good at making non-urgent, but important, things happen.

They don't have a clear, compelling introduction. Having a practiced introduction you are comfortable with boosts your confidence and makes starting interesting conversations much easier.

They feel they're not "naturally good" at networking for some reason. Even people who look "natural" feel some apprehension with strangers. Here's the dirty secret: people who are shy or quiet-spoken can leave stronger first impressions (because they are better listeners).

Invest your time differently and get dramatic results

Our recommendation is that you up your networking by a factor of five or ten. Importantly, this will not increase the total amount of time you spend in job-search mode; rather, it will shift it from unproductive activities (sending too many generic applications) to more productive activities (research, effective outreach, and follow-up). In the next section, we show you how to do that, and how to make your networking more effective by applying modern science and a dose of personal discipline.

Agencies, recruiters, and selection software

A book about the job market isn't complete without mentioning employment agencies, recruiters, and the software packages HR organizations use to sort through thousands of resumes they receive every year. While each has a place in the job searcher's world, you shouldn't focus on them in order to beat the odds. Here's why:

- **Employment agencies** work on behalf of employers (often for government departments) to fill specific skills-based roles. These roles are usually temporary (anywhere from two weeks to a year), meaning the hiring organization is not looking for a long-term fit, just someone short term with basic skills. These jobs usually are lower paying with few benefits, and the agency that placed you takes a portion of your pay. Don't dismiss these roles altogether, but be selective and develop specific criteria (refer to Stage 3 of this section) for pursuing and accepting temporary roles.

- **Recruiters** are engaged by organizations to help them identify and place top talent. Recruiters are usually paid only when they are successful and typically charge the organization a one-time fee of about 25%–30% of the role's annual salary. If your profile matches a role they are actively trying to fill, recruiters become your new best friends, and they work with you to help you land the job. If the hiring company rejects you, your resume goes back into their database awaiting another client opportunity that might match your profile. Make sure local recruiters know about you and have an updated copy of your resume on file. They usually only contact you if they have a need; don't waste time trying to get their attention. Recruiters are not receptive, so focus your efforts elsewhere.

- **Selection software** is used by many medium-sized and large organizations because of the volume of applications they receive. This software runs applications searching for specific (customized) words and rejects all applications that don't contain those words; as the number of applications increases, organizations adjust their search criteria to decrease the number of applications that filter through. Some applicants pad their resumes and cover letters with more and more buzzwords (regardless of accuracy or appropriateness) to try to filter through successfully. The bottom line: this is a futile activity and entails a lot of wasted effort for both parties. Your time is better spent developing effective networking opportunities.

Step 1: Confirm your career search time budget

Our advice about stepping up your networking activities holds, whether you are currently in a full-time job search or can only commit limited time to exploring career options. What follows are some general ideas about how much time you should be spending on your search depending on your status.

Full-time job search:

Finding a career is your main priority, so you need to stay alert and active. Spend at least two hours a day researching and attending three or four networking events a week. Keep your pipeline (more on this in Stage 3) as full as possible, and maintain high contact rates. **Active job seekers should be committing to a minimum of 25 hours a week** for all career networking and opportunity development activities.

Time-constrained job seekers:

This includes currently employed individuals, students about to graduate, and people trying to reenter the workforce after a long absence. Since you have limited time and availability to develop and work your network, a good strategy is to build up and maintain ongoing momentum in your networking activities for several months (we recommend four to six months to lay the groundwork) **before** you are planning to enter/reenter the working world. As a rule of thumb, you should be attempting to contact two new people per week to build your network connections. Maintaining this level of disciplined networking takes **about four to five hours per week.**

Full-time contractor/consultant:

For ongoing success, you need to actively network for a few hours many times weekly, if not daily. Factor in about three to four hours per week to attend networking events and two to three more hours per week researching others, reaching out, and working your pipeline. That is a total of **about five to seven hours per week,** or around 15% of a typical 40-hour workweek.

A Day in the Life of a Full-Time Job Seeker

What follows is a daily ritual for a fully engaged full-time job seeker. While everyone should create a schedule that works for them and their particular situation, the key point is that there are a number of things that one needs to do everyday to maintain health, motivation, enthusiasm and momentum.

6:00 am	out of bed
6:00 - 7:00 am	daily exercise or meditation
7:00 - 7:30 am	wash, dress, breakfast
7:30 am	start "work day"
7:30 - 8:30 am	research new opportunities (lists, newspapers, LinkedIn, etc.)
8:30 - 9:00 am	scrub opportunity pipeline, follow-up emails and calls
10:00 - 10:30 am	first Exploration Meeting (pre-arranged, often virtual)
10:30 - 11:00 am	notes, follow-up actions, reflection
11:00 am	break for lunch, stretch, other activities
12:30 pm	restart work day
1:00 - 1:30 pm	2nd (pre-arranged) Exploration Meeting
1:30 - 2:00 pm	notes, follow-up actions, reflection
2:00 - 4:00 pm	work related activities (cover letters, RFP's, research)
4:00 pm	end structured "work day" activities
4:00 - 6:00 pm	light exercise (for example walking), journaling, family errands
6:00 pm	dinner with family (or friends) – talk about your progress!
7:30 pm	attend networking event (2 to 3 per week)
9:00 - 10:00 pm	recreational reading
10:00 pm	lights out... A good night's sleep for the demands of tomorrow!

Stage 2: The Science of Networks and Human Connection

We have suggested a radical shift in how people approach looking for or changing jobs: a five- to ten-fold increase in networking and a similar decrease in the “spray and pray” approach. We first justified this notion by showing that most good jobs go to candidates on an “inside track” (preferred candidates). Now we are going to further substantiate this recommendation through exploring some of the science behind human connections. The general science also has a lot to suggest about **how** you should approach networking.

Neurochemistry and human connections: Neurochemistry can influence our behavior and play an important role in networking and interacting with people. The best-known neuroactive substances are cortisol, serotonin, and oxytocin. Cortisol is a “stress” chemical that invokes our flight-or-flight behavior when a threat is perceived; oxytocin and serotonin are associated with closeness and feeling good. When you network **and focus on the connection,** you create a positive experience for the other person that lowers his or her cortisol levels (stress) and raises serotonin and oxytocin levels (safety, support, friendship). Focusing exclusively on “what this person can do for me” (a transactional relationship) does the opposite.

> ***Network insight #1:*** *Seek to put people at ease. Reduce their stress levels by making it easy for them to help you, and increase their social engagement by encouraging them to share their interests, opinions, and insights with you. Plan your initial approach and introduction with this in mind.*

Chaos theory and finding jobs you didn’t know existed: The second bit of science that affects your networking success is chaos theory. Chaos theory, attributed to meteorologist Edward Lorenz, contends that distant, seemingly insignificant, and unconnected events can lead to a major change: the now-famous “butterfly effect.” The implication is that we cannot know with certainty how an interaction may or may not cause a positive “chain reaction” for us. For example, Paul has found consulting gigs through people who aren’t themselves buyers, including a very young administrative assistant (who worked for a CEO and was looking for a coach).

> ***Network insight #2:*** *At networking events, let luck work for you. You rarely know in advance “who knows who” because of the*

seemingly random nature of personal networks. Meet as many people as you can, and be magnanimous and warm-hearted with them all!

Six degrees of separation: Six degrees of separation is the theory that everyone and everything in the world is six or fewer steps away. For networking purposes, according to this theory, we are only six conversations away from an available opportunity. This tells us that while the optimal chain of end-to-end connections ("How many people/steps from me to get to Bill Gates?") is never more than six steps, the challenge is, "Which six people do I have to go through?"

> ***Network insight #3:*** *As with insight #2, it is difficult to predict who knows who and how the network works. Connect with as many people as you can while still maintaining depth of interaction.*

It's not what or who you know: The mantra "It's not what you know, but who you know" stresses the importance of networking and reinforces the notion that skills are less important than connections. The key question is: ***"Who knows me, and what do they know about me?"*** If you know somebody who doesn't know or remember you, how is that helpful? And if someone knows you in a different context than the powerful tagline you developed, how does that help you? You have two objectives to focus on: **who** knows you (directly correlated with your own outreach activities), and **what** they know about you (strongly influenced by the impact of your message).

> ***Network insight #4:*** *You can strongly influence* ***who*** *knows you and* ***what*** *they know about you through delivering a clear message in all your outreach activities. You want each contact to retain at least one thing that makes the conversation memorable; work to get the key messages we crafted in Section 2 naturally woven into your introductions and conversations.*

Weak and strong connections: In 1973, American sociologist Mark Granovetter published "The Strength of Weak Ties," which has become a highly influential and widely cited study. Granovetter interviewed dozens of people to find out how they used social networks to land new jobs, and discovered most jobs were found through **weak acquaintances. Weaker** social ties can actually improve our chances of finding opportunities more so than stronger ties. Since our stronger connections tend to move in the same circles as us, we may already share the same information.

Acquaintances, by contrast, know people we do not, and thus have additional information.

> ***Network insight #5:*** *Expand your networking activities beyond your typical peer groups. More diverse networks are a greater source of novel information and new contacts, which in turn introduces more opportunities.*

Networking tool #1: Managing the networking event

Understanding these basic insights and how they relate to each other will help you develop and nurture a strong network. Here are 10 tips based upon those insights.

1. **Practice your tagline and brand with every conversation.** This will make you more comfortable with presenting yourself that way.

2. **Get genuinely curious and ask lots of questions.** You will acquire new information, which will provide you a more comprehensive understanding of the world around you.

3. **Build and strengthen your new networking connections.** You now have a broader network, and each member of your network has a reasonable understanding of you—your passion, your caliber, and your future goals. You also need to keep nurturing those connections through finding ways to share your value with them.

4. **Continue to reach out and meet new people.** Doing this provides further data, feedback, and confidence you can use to evolve and tighten your brand messaging, enhance your conversational skills, and improve how you present yourself to others.

5. **Approach someone else who is alone.** Others may also feel uncomfortable and stressed, so going over and introducing yourself will help them (and you) to relax and possibly stop the release of cortisol (stress) and get the oxytocin (social bonding) flowing instead.

6. **The objective is not to land a job; the purpose is to connect.** Most people you meet won't have a job for you, and if they think that is your main objective, then they will get more stressed

(remember cortisol, from earlier?). Be honest about your intentions (ultimately to discover a great opportunity); however, be clear that you don't expect them to have one or know of one.

7. **Ask about their favorite subject—them!** Most people enjoy sharing their stories, and listening rather than sharing your own demonstrates that you are interested. There is an old story about two famously charismatic British Prime Ministers: "When you talked to Disraeli, you felt he was the most interesting person in the world; when you talked to Gladstone, you thought you were!" Try to be like Gladstone to make yourself more memorable.

8. **Always follow up!** If you talked for more than a few minutes, always drop a "good to meet you" email. Always. It is both courteous **and** jogs their memory about you and your interaction.

9. **Periodically "drip-feed" your growing network with interesting articles or connections.** Your contacts will appreciate the information and keep you in mind. The information you share should be specific to their issues and interests, which you know from your conversations with them.

10. **Don't give up on your network contacts if they don't respond immediately.** People are busy; have patience. In our view, if they don't respond to one "ping," it is usually worth one (or several) more attempts over the next few weeks. While there is a very fine line between persistence and stalking, most people fail by not being persistent and patient enough with their follow ups.

Step 1: Schedule events and start prepping—now!

1. Schedule **at least** three group networking sessions for the next several weeks. If you don't know of any, do your homework. (Google is your new best friend.) Most networking events are free; formally register and commit yourself to attending.

2. Review the do's and don'ts and jot down bullet points in your journal that cover the following:

Your introductory opening (keep it short and crisp);

What are you going to say after your introduction (how to turn the conversation over to the other person);

Decide what your follow-up preferences are (email, phone call, LinkedIn, etc.) in advance, and write out a line or two asking for permission to follow up and share your communication method. For example, this is a good time to mention you write a regular newsletter and ask the person's permission to subscribe to it;

Write out some ideas about what your "drip-feeding" value into your network connections might look like. Think about the kind of material you regularly consume (articles, TED Talks, etc.) and how frequently you might be able to share this with them;

List out specific objectives for your conversations. Your general objectives should include:

Testing and tightening your basic introduction

Finding out general interests of your networking partner

Gaining some insights on their work environment (industry, role, focus)

Inquiring as to their recommendations for other people/organizations you should be contacting

Finding out if they are receptive to periodic follow-up requests from you

Networking tool #2: The Exploration Meeting

Exploration Meetings are the other important networking tool. At heart, an Exploration Meeting is nothing more than a conversation between two people to: a) build rapport and trust by sharing stories, and b) exchange ideas. You will want to have a lot of these meetings with people you meet at networking events. You want to seize the chance to cement a new, and potentially beneficial, relationship.

Why should new contacts meet with you? As social animals, most people want to help others and enjoy sharing their story. We are both tenured businessmen, and **almost never say no** to someone who wants a quick 20-minute connect (when they are positioned effectively). **Conversely, people almost never say yes** to a meeting when you have an overt sales (or employment) agenda. The world of work is a world of people. The job market is not an impersonal conglomerate of machines and statistics, but a vast network of interrelated human beings. They know this too, and if they are competent, they are keen to expand **their network** also.

You should be able to easily meet with people junior to you; after all, they want to connect with more senior people for the reasons mentioned in this book. Connecting with peers is similarly easy: most people enjoy sharing the ups and downs of work with someone in a similar role. Connecting with senior people can be trickier (this is a true-but-sad fact: humans are hierarchical primates). Generally, if you feel you hit it off with someone at a level more senior than you, suggest meeting for coffee or lunch. If you do not particularly connect, still fire off a thank-you email. Perhaps after a second chance meeting, a planned meeting might seem more appropriate.

Your natural shyness may stand in your way. (For pre-human mammals, rejection by the herd meant you became someone's dinner; evolutionary biology makes us all somewhat shy because of this fear of rejection.) Go meet new people anyhow; remember, we are suggesting what may be an increase of five- or ten-fold in your networking. This will take sustained effort on your part (or insistent nudging from a trusted friend). The who, what, where, when, and how of the **Exploration Meeting** is as follows:

Who: Have these meetings with people that you have just met to get to know them better, and to put your relationship on a more professional footing. Since you have done so much work on your brand and positioning in the previous section, you also want to test-drive the "new you" with people you know a bit better.

What: These can be very, very informal, or more formal, depending on you (your industry and standard business dress), and them (the way they show up at work). Meeting for coffee is less formal than having lunch. Having lunch is less formal than meeting them at their office.

When: We suggest two or three of these a week if you are fully employed (but seeking a change). If you are not working, you should have two or three a day (for the reasons we suggested before: your timescales are more urgent, and it combats the isolation and mood swings of unemployment). These meetings may be as short as 20 minutes long, and never (we recommend) longer than 40 minutes.

How: Never ask for a job or even offer your résumé, unless they suggest it. Spend most of the meeting listening, and convey your story concisely (so they "get the point" of you.) Make offers to connect them with other people who may be useful. Use reverse thinking; according to thousands of job seekers and numerous international research project results, the fastest way to get a job is never to ask for one. The quickest way to get a tip as a server is to never ask for one; conversely, the worst way for the server to get a tip is to ask for one. Let the other individual decide to be generous; that is, to remain in control of the decision process.

Constructing effective Exploration Meetings

Exploration Meetings are similar to business meetings and should be conducted as such, with you spearheading the effort. It is helpful to consider the Exploration Meeting as a process with the five components outlined below:

1. **Build rapport, set the meeting agenda, and define the purpose.** You want to create a roadmap for the interviewee with a sense of direction and purpose for the meeting. Recognize that the individual may be uncertain or uncomfortable, not knowing your motives or exactly what is about to happen. Explain your intentions, plans, and expectations so the individual clearly understands why you are interested in meeting and the agenda. Emphasize that you are researching the market for your own career to determine where your skills might apply, and you are seeking that person's expertise. By laying out the purpose and protocol of the Exploration Meeting, you are establishing rapport. Get to know the people you are meeting with. Ask them interesting questions about their industries, and let them talk. You reap what you sew; your attitude toward them will be reflected back by them to you.

2. **Review the industry and obtain background information.** Study the organization beforehand—read the company website or other data to learn about who you are meeting with and his or her industry. Only supply your résumé if it is requested in advance. Do not send it unsolicited, because a résumé is associated with a job request, which conflicts with your message of not expecting the other person to have a job opening. Provide a brief self-introduction (your tagline), and reiterate your meeting request is based on a two-phase career search and this is the information-gathering process. Refer to the person who recommended you for this meeting, offering up a positive

connection: "Mr. Jones thinks very highly of you." Report briefly on people whom you have already met to gain their insights, either at this time or preferably at the wrap-up.

3. **Facilitate the dialogue.** The dual objectives of giving and receiving information lies within your hands, especially on receiving information. Definitely respond to questions asked of you, but preparing your own questions in advance will help you manage the discussion. If you are amazed at what you learn, you will probably have conducted a successful meeting. Remember to be sincere when asking for advice and information, which acknowledges the other person's expertise. Such recognition will prompt the individual to want to help you. To facilitate the dialogue, keep the meeting focused on your agenda, watch the agenda timing, listen, and probe attentively. Ask each person you meet different questions.

4. **Close the meeting and decide the next step.** This is the point at which you want to confirm that the outcome of the meeting will grow your networking opportunities. If you haven't received additional referrals, take steps to trigger suggested future contacts, perhaps by sharing the names of some companies with whom you would like to meet. Remember that one good referral is better than ten mediocre ones. Continue building your network by obtaining one or more further referrals from your Exploration Meetings. Together, clarify what pending actions have resulted from the meeting. What are your tasks? What are the other person's tasks? Make sure your triggers are not suggestions. The list of companies you plan to visit is a trigger; asking directly for referrals is not. Reminding your interviewee that you would appreciate being informed if a contact person should come to mind is a trigger; asking him or her to be on the watch for you is not.

5. **Follow up.** Ask the interviewees for permission to keep them informed of your progress and then observe the response. If it is less than enthusiastic, reverse the suggestion nicely ("Or should I leave it for you to check with me?"). Most will appreciate being kept informed. They then have an undeclared stake in your success, and will want you to prosper. Write a brief thank-you letter within 24 hours.

Getting referrals from Exploration Meeting

We advise you not to directly ask for referrals during your Exploration Meeting to avoid placing pressure on the other person. Instead, we suggest you develop a list of individuals and companies with whom you plan to meet, and use that list to seek more referrals.

If the meeting ends without any referrals, there is a step you can take without offending the other person. In fact, we recommend this step even if you do get referrals from the meeting.

At the end of the meeting, but only after your host has finished talking, thank the person for the information. Then, suggest you will be meeting with others. Present the list (visual is more significant than verbal) and say: "As you probably realize, I plan to meet other people to gather information, such as the information you have provided. Here is a list of my targeted companies. What is your opinion about this list?"The reason you wait until end of the meeting is to not pre-empt potential referrals the person was going to share.

If the person recognizes the companies and knows someone you can talk to, thank the person and ask, "May I mention your name when I contact her?"

We strongly recommend that you practice your approach so that you are comfortable and the session flows organically. Remember to use your own words and style, speaking in a way that is natural for you.

Step 2: Schedule some Exploration Meetings now!

Now that you know more about Exploration Meetings, start scheduling them! Get out your journal again and:

List at least five people you want to meet with to gain information relevant to your particular interests and search criteria. You don't need specific names just yet; you can list industry roles ("I want to speak with someone who handles Cloud Computing support for a Fortune 500 company") or skill sets. Once you have determined who you want to meet with, go on LinkedIn and search for anyone in your immediate network that can help you make a desired connection. If your LinkedIn network is currently underdeveloped, search the internet with the same criteria and see what you can find.

Write down names that pop up on your LinkedIn and research more about them and their organizations. This research will help inform the kinds of questions you can expect them to resonate with.

Develop a set of questions for your meetings.

Develop a brief meeting agenda.

Write out a basic script for the meeting. Try not to be overly prescriptive, as the actual meeting may unfold differently than you expected. Be flexible and let the meeting content flow, but also make sure your major agenda items are covered.

Finally, email them now, or if short on time, schedule a time when you will do so.

Step 3: Read, summarize, then practice, practice, practice

This is a lot of information to digest, so our final recommended step in this stage is to read and reread this information and summarize the main points in your journal. Review the summary regularly as part of your ongoing preparation in advance of specific networking activities. And of course, practice! At first, putting some of these tips into action will seem foreign and possibly uncomfortable to you, but with practice and time, these will become automatic, powerful, and positive behaviors.

Stage 3: How to Manage and Progress Opportunities

So far, we've examined how the job market really operates and the criticality of discovering opportunities before they are even advertised (Stage 1). We showed you how to become a preferred candidate during the formal process through building personal network connections based on familiarity and trust. Touching on the scientific principles at work in networks and human connections, we detailed out effective networking tactics for both group events and Exploration Meetings (Stage 2). Our overall recommendation is to dedicate 80% of your job-search time to networking activities and only 20% of your time sending résumés to posted positions. This switch in focus will likely require a five- to ten-fold increase in networking activity.

This stage looks more closely at how you can put this all together into ongoing action through developing and managing that network so it produces gold. You will want to convert casual connections to deeper ones, and connections to opportunities, opportunities to concrete applications, applications will lead to interviews (shorthand for some kind of formal, mutual evaluation), and (finally) you will have to negotiate terms. This process is shown in the diagram below.

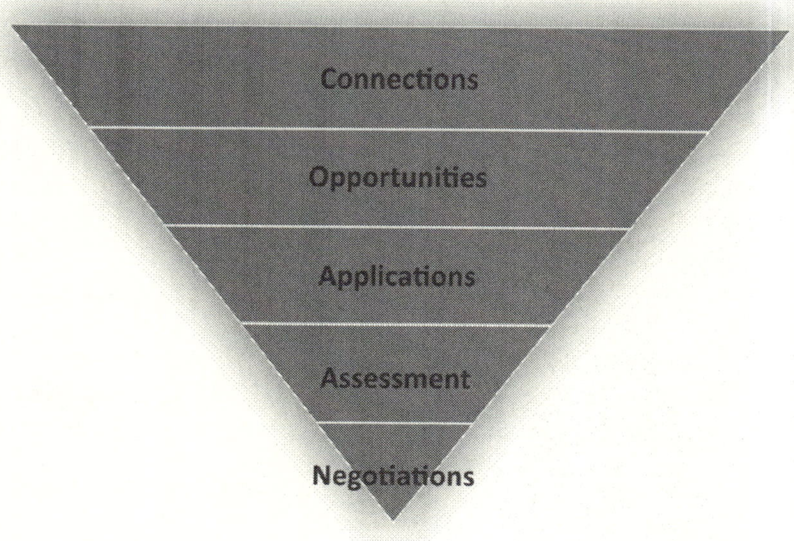

This is a lot to keep track of, and we are going to suggest a means of doing so that serious job hunters and job changers can readily manage their progress.

This funnel is like a salesperson's: there are many prospects at the top, and few at the bottom. Your job is to: a) fill the funnel at the top continuously, and b) transition evolving opportunities down the funnel, making them increasingly tangible and real.

Over time, you will remove potential contacts (i.e., dead ends, unanswered connection requests, no common ground discovered, no opportunities that meet your interests), and some will eventually evolve into something worthwhile (a full-time job, paid project, collaborative activity, volunteer gig, etc.).

In the meantime, there might be as many as 100 connections you are "working." You will want to keep track of whom you have met, what actions you have taken, and what the next steps are.

Step 1: Creating a "pipeline" spreadsheet

On the first tab of your spreadsheet, you will want a list of connections you are "working"; that is, trying to develop into a concrete job (or gig if you prefer). Next to the name, you want to include pertinent information: company, contact details, and perhaps when and where you last met.

Action: Create this list now! It won't yet be complete, but you will have started it.

You are now going to do what every good salesperson does: "qualify" the opportunity that this connection represents. By that we mean assessing whether it is worth nurturing. While the answer to this question is different for everybody, there are several categories of opportunities that are applicable to most people, such as the following:

1. Pursuing a posted, available role (from a job board);
2. Pursuing an Exploration Meeting with a targeted individual;
3. A volunteer position where you can learn something new (skills, sector, people);
4. A contract position (fixed time frame) that aligns with your interests and skill set;

5. A pro-bono speaking event or educational experience where you can showcase your knowledge;

6. An upcoming event where you have a specific goal to achieve, or a course (training) you are considering attending.

7. A collaborative project with someone (or group) that will further your objectives;

Action: On the next column of your spreadsheet, describe the kind of opportunity that you might create through this connection. Use the seven categories listed above as a starting point; add further category types if necessary.

Next, you need to evaluate these opportunities (the second tier of your funnel).

Step 2: Assessing relevant opportunities

Once you have decided which types of opportunities to pursue, you need to establish specific criteria to consider opportunities that start to appear from your networking activities. Each of your categories should have some precise, predetermined assessment criteria to help you select worthwhile opportunities. Refer back to Section 1 when you created your vision, mission, and values. In reviewing that work, think of whether or how specific opportunities might further your purpose. Here are some ideas to help you develop a more detailed filter for each of your categories.

1. **Pursuing a posted, available role:**

Establish firm criteria about your expectations: salary, benefits, vacation, flexibility, travel, work-at-home expectations, working environment, etc.;

Use these criteria when applying for any job, whether or not the opportunity came from a job board or a networking connection;

These criteria are vital for evaluating a position, whether it is a good fit, what you need to be comfortable, and what tradeoffs you are willing to make. The best time to do this is when you are thinking clearly and objectively, not during the negotiation process.

Finally, keep in mind that you are most likely competing with many others for this job. If you discovered the opportunity via a job board, your chances of getting an interview are miniscule. Reach out to your network and seek out people inside the company who can put in a good word for you. This might entail asking someone you know well to put in a good word for you with the hiring manager, or asking a more casual acquaintance if he or she thinks you would be a good fit for the role, and if so, whether he or she might be willing to mention you favorably to the hiring manager. In working to advance these types of opportunities, focus your efforts working toward influencing the hiring manager, not HR.

2. **Pursuing an Exploration Meeting with a targeted individual:**

   Your criteria here will focus on how much effort you are prepared to put into pursuing a meeting before you give up and remove this opportunity from your pipeline.

   Most people are receptive to having a meeting; the biggest challenge is trying to get their attention (phone, email, voicemail, LinkedIn request, etc.) in the first place and then arranging a convenient meeting time.

   Base your criteria on a combination of elapsed time and contact attempts. For example, you might give yourself six weeks to connect up with someone via an initial email, followed by a phone call one week later, then reverting back to email, etc. as you work through your six-week window.

   While each attempt only takes you a few minutes, eventually the non-respondents start to clog up your pipeline and need to be removed. Your criteria will help with this.

3. **A volunteer position where you can learn something new (skills, sector, people):**

   Volunteering is an excellent way to learn new things, practice new skills, meet new people, and learn firsthand about a new sector or industry. When assessing these opportunities, use these questions as your criteria:

   What will you learn?

Who will you meet and work with? How is that relevant and complementary to your bigger career objectives?

How much time will it take both daily and weekly? Can you commit that time without severely impacting your other networking and job-seeking objectives?

If you decide to include volunteering in your opportunity pipeline, make sure your criteria is definite—this will help you select the right opportunities.

4. **A contract position (fixed time frame) that aligns with your interests and skill set:**

You may come across existing contract opportunities that are attractive to you. These are typically presented as a Request for Proposal (RFP), when the organization provides general context to a situation they would like addressed, and request numerous interested parties to submit bids.

Remember when we mentioned many posted jobs already have a preferred candidate (Section 3, Stage 1)? Well, most formal RFPs have a "preferred contractor" who has a much greater chance of landing the work than other responders.

In pursuing this opportunity, if you are asked to submit an RFP and you know little about the organization or don't know anyone within the company, recognize that your chances of landing the project are very small.

Alternately, if a decision-maker in your network—whom you have had recent and positive interactions with—requests the RFP, this may make *you* the preferred contractor. In this case, you definitely want to take this request seriously and submit a well-thought out, thorough proposal for their consideration.

5. **A pro-bono speaking event or educational experience where you can showcase your knowledge:**

A relevant example from coauthor Tim: *"I currently maintain an opportunity pipeline of 30 active slots; that means that assuming my pipeline is at 80% full, I always have 24 conversations (relationships) under development at any time. One of my categories is pro-bono speaking gigs. Over the past six months or so, I have received requests for more and more gigs. Recently, I decided that I was too heavily invested in pro-bono gigs and so created some new criteria for my filter. I decided to only pursue shorter speaking gigs (60 minutes or less) with an expected audience of 30 or more, with a maximum of three gigs in my pipeline at any given time (10% of the 30 available slots). Those criteria are somewhat fluid, and I use them as a guideline to help me quickly determine whether an opportunity is worth pursuing. Going forward, I intend to adjust my criteria accordingly if anything becomes less relevant or too restrictive."*

6. **An upcoming event or training opportunity where you have specific goals:**

Potential events you should attend include industry networking events, new Meetup groups (check out http://meetup.com for your particular region), local conferences, and the like.

In your chosen field, there are many skills development courses you can explore. In addition to those delivered in your location, also check out virtual options, and MOOC's (massively open online courses).

Set some criteria for what a "successful" event or training course means to you. This might include learning something relevant from a keynote presentation, meeting a specific number of new people you can follow up with (and possibly seek follow-up Exploration Meetings), adding a new skill, or experimenting with and testing out a new message.

Only keep this opportunity on your pipeline until you have decided whether or not to attend. If you are attending and have registered, then move it to your agenda as an upcoming commitment and remove it from the pipeline. If you are not attending, take it off your pipeline to free up a slot.

7. **A collaborative project with someone (or group) that will further your objectives:**

You may decide to collaborate with someone and write a book, start a podcast series, or develop a new training course. This might be someone in your local network, or, as in the case of Paul and Tim, someone you connected with through social media.

Your criteria here will be about fit, time involvement, perceived competencies, etc. Collaborative projects usually consist of numerous conversations and unfold over many months. It might also cycle through your pipeline in various guises, as the nature and form or your collaborative project morphs to accommodate the emerging realities of your life and that of your collaborator.

If this opportunity becomes "stuck," isn't progressing, and starts to clog up your pipeline, don't hesitate to remove it. Make a note to yourself in your agenda to check back in three months and reinvestigate the respective levels of interest in the project.

The pipeline you have created helps you develop, advance, and establish two different kinds of opportunities: unpaid activities that align with your interests and further your career goals, and paid assignments.

Converting unpaid activities:

If you work your opportunity pipeline effectively, it will likely turn some opportunities into deals, and unpaid activities are the easiest to convert. In the case of pro-bono speaking gigs or securing volunteer positions, these will be straightforward and don't require much more work on your part (other than actually fulfilling whatever commitment you make). Another category of unpaid opportunities involves collaboration projects with others. Moving these forward requires you and your collaborator to adhere to basic project management principles to accomplish your established goals.

Converting contract opportunities:

Paid work assignments that transition from opportunities into firm deals come in two basic forms: traditional employment agreements and fixed time frame contracts. Organizations are increasingly offering short-term contracts over full-time employment, as their initial risk is less and the internal decision process is usually quicker. When deciding whether to accept an offered contract, consider the following:

Is it likely the initial contract might lead to the chance of longer-term employment (or extended contracts)?

Will it still allow you to continue to pursue other opportunities that might ultimately lead to better opportunities?

Does this contract fulfill some important aspect of your overall career objective(s)?

In most cases, taking on a short-term contract that supports one or more immediate objectives is a good step in your overall career progression, and does not limit your ability to continue exploring other opportunities.

Converting employment opportunities:

Formal employment opportunities require you to submit your application through the appropriate channel so it will proceed through the official intake and selection process (Section 1, Stage 1). This may be a role that you have discovered through your own research and are pursuing actively, or maybe you found the role through your networking activities and the hiring manager (or other key influencer) asked you to formally apply for the job. Regardless of how you learned about the role, you still need to follow the hiring organization's official application process. This process will likely involve an online web form and submission process, or it might be the more traditional method of sending your résumé and a detailed cover letter. We discussed the résumé development process in Section 2; depending on the organization's application process requirements, you may have to tweak your two-page résumé format, or cut and paste the appropriate information from your master résumé into their online form. Share the same story you developed in Section 2: the 'real you.' Additionally, you usually need to draft and provide a cover letter as part of the formal application package. Your overall application package, **and specifically the cover letter,** should convey the following:

Confirm you are a good fit:

Respond to all the important criteria in the job description, describe why you are an excellent candidate, and convey your interest.

Be thorough, concise, and punctual:

Traditional business RFPs are tendered by major organizations when seeking competitive services or products. Service providers competing for this business must march to the beat of the company's drum and respond meticulously when submitting their proposal. Company representatives who assess RFPs will award points on each component and deduct points for those that are ignored or have an invalid response.

View your response as seriously as the company does. In our scenario, the RFP is your overall application package. In business, if a bid arrives even one minute late or does not address all the requested items, it is disqualified. Likewise, you must first find out the due date (and the due hour if applicable) for submission, and then observe the submission requirements to the letter.

Show you meet every important criterion:

Your cover letter is meant to confirm that you meet (or surpass) all the qualifications. The only way to show that clearly is to list the company's criterion and describe specifically how you meet each one (detailed in coming pages).

Bring out relevant information to the job that is not contained in your résumé:

Your résumé cannot possibly contain your entire history. Writing a tailored cover letter forces you to remember past experiences that may be pertinent to the employer's criterion. Laying out your qualifications in a simple, two-column table format will leave no doubt of your potential fit. Respond to each criterion, regardless of simplicity.

Make it easy for the employer to relate your qualifications to the job requirements:

Companies spend a lot of time and money on advertising, hiring someone to design the ad and select the proper wording. Be sure to address the words and phrasing used in the ad. Often, 'gatekeepers' are assigned to screen applications and to award points for each item having a positive response. Your failure to acknowledge a certain point because it is implied in other parts of your submission will leave you without a mark for that criterion.

Your cover letter phrases must follow exactly the same order as those in the advertisement; otherwise, you may be viewed as noncompliant to their stated requirements.

Leave nothing to interpretation:

By not addressing all areas of the job specification directly, you risk the reader misinterpreting your words. He or she might miss the connection between your résumé and the criterion altogether, or might not clearly understand whether you fit or not. When in doubt, the reader will err on the side of caution and assume you do not qualify.

Step 3: Managing formal applications and interviews

On the next tab of your spreadsheet, make a list of applications for jobs (or gigs, or projects) that "go formal." You will want information of what was sent to whom, on what date, and what expected follow-up date. Typically, you will want to chase applications that have not been responded to after about two weeks (unless you have been specifically told a longer period). You will want the names of any other connections you have in the business; not just HR, but any people that you know internally. Generally, you will want to let them know you are in discussions, but use your judgment—there may be sound political reasons to not let them know.

You'll also want to keep track of everyone you interview with, and whether you have followed up with a note of thanks. It goes without saying that all interviews, or all meetings with prospective employers (or clients) should be followed up with a thank-you note. On this spreadsheet, or in your journal, make sure you jot down any questions you might have.

Step 4: Submitting formal applications (cover letter and résumé)

When responding to formal employment opportunities, you must follow a specific order of steps to advance a potential role to a formal job offer. The first of these are:

Fine-tuning your résumé to match the posted opportunity;

Constructing an impressive cover letter for your application;

Formally submitting your application within the stated deadline.

Fine tune your résumé

In Section 2, we touched upon how to create your model résumé from your master résumé. While we strongly recommend you adjust your résumé as little as possible, you do have to customize your résumé for each position you apply for. You cannot send the same résumé to every job because every job requirement is unique. Follow these guidelines in your fine-tuning work:

Match your **Opportunity Sought** section to the objective advertised (without stretching your abilities);

Ensure your **Capabilities** have a corresponding adjustment to complement your Opportunity Sought statement;

Select six or seven **Accomplishments** (from the overall inventory you created in Section 2) that best fit the requirement.

Below is an example of the revised *Opportunity Sought* and Capabilities statements. Your master résumé might read as follows:

Opportunity Sought: *To direct and operate a mid- to large-sized company or department involved in the development and distribution of goods or services in IT or another sector. To be involved in the business planning and development of that company with the goal of improving its operational and financial positions.*

Capabilities:

Five years as vice president and senior sales executive for a $6 billion multinational software company.

Eight years as director and senior manager of two major Federal government IT operations in departments employing more than 30,000 people.

Two years as CEO in a startup company developing and deploying IT products and services. Focused on business management.

The **advertised position** you are formally applying to states:

Wanted: President and CEO of a growing technology company in the biotech sector with demonstrated results in planning and managing successful product developments with an ability to liaise with key stakeholders: investors, board of directors, community leaders, and staff.

Here is how your fine-tuned statements might read; adjustments are shown <u>**in underlined bold**</u>.

Opportunity Sought*: To direct and operate a* <u>***dynamic***</u>*, mid- to large-sized company (delete: or department) involved in the development and distribution of* <u>***technology***</u> *(replaces IT) goods or services. To be involved in the business planning and development of that company with the goal of* *improving its operational and financial position* ***and utilize my relationship management skills****.*

Capabilities:

Five years as vice president and senior sales executive for a $6 billion multinational software company.

Eight years as director and senior manager of two major Federal government ***technology*** *operations in departments employing more than 30,000 people.*

Two years as CEO in a startup company developing and deploying IT products and services. Focused on business management.

Twenty years successfully managing relationships with investors, founders, boards of directors, suppliers, communities-at-large, and specific employee groups as large as 3,000.

Write your cover letter

We recommend a two-column format table for your cover letter. Include the appropriate number of rows to respond to each criterion of the job specification. Respond not only to the job specification, but also to other portions of the ad, such as the general job description. For example:

Your job requirement	My fit to your requirement
Will involve considerable international travel	Spent four years on assignments in Chile, Mexico, Spain, and the United States (Washington, D.C.)

Don't paraphrase; write out the full description. When you are finished, the left-hand column should detail the full advertisement. Don't worry about the length of your responses; for now, concentrate on addressing each requirement. Don't just repeat the job requirement in your response; instead, provide concrete, numerical examples:

Wrong

Your job requirement	My fit to your requirement
Must have a demostrated facility with high-level computer languages such as C+	Have a demostrated facility with high-level computer languages such as C+ and C++

Right

Your job requirement	My fit to your requirement
Must have a demostrated facility with high-level computer languages such as C+	Spent six years writing code in C+, C++ and C sharp on high-visibility commercial software applications for Corel Corporation, a leading international software company

Treat your résumé and cover letter as independent documents. When drafting a cover letter, it's tempting to take a shortcut by telling yourself a certain specification is already covered in your résumé. While this may be, your résumé and cover letter are often separated as they move through the assessment chain. Treat your cover letter as a stand-alone and complete document. Be thorough and rigorous.

Pay attention to the length of your cover letter. A lengthy response will bore the reviewer and not be read. Try to keep your cover letter to no more than two pages. At the same time, be mindful your cover letter is thorough. You must find the balance between length and content. If you do not respond thoroughly to a criterion, you may miss being scored for that item.

In developing a response to a posted role, note the following:

Begin your letter with a brief overview of your background as it relates to the position. It should come from the substance of your Opportunity Sought statement, but not digress from the advertised need;

Verify the headings for the two columns are on both pages;

End the letter with a conclusion, your résumé, and an action item that you will take in relation to this application;

After you officially submit your application, contact the organization and confirm your application was received.

Step 5: Prepping for formal interviews

The job interview is the beginning of the end goal of landing the job. It has to be conducted in such a way as to optimize your chances of being selected for the position. You cannot change the way the interviewer thinks, but you can move the process as much in your favor as possible. Therefore, in the end, you want to guarantee you have done everything possible. Some advice:

Be prepared:

Bring an extra copy of your résumé to the interview.

Know how to describe the essence of you in one minute.

Think of short answers to interview questions you might struggle with ("What is your biggest weakness?"; "Where do you see yourself in five years?").

Brainstorm good questions to ask (relevant to the role and company).

Rehearse the interview process with a trusted confidant.

Make sure your outfit is presentable (no wrinkles, holes, etc.).

Appreciate the interviewers' concerns: Interviewers usually voice several concerns about applicants: namely, poor communication skills; exaggeration of qualifications; lateness; poor grooming habits; lack of honesty of responses or an unwillingness to delve into past work experiences, and treating their questions as irrelevant. Keep these in mind while you are planning your interview strategy and approach.

Be on time. Arrive early; give yourself time in case you get caught in traffic. Make sure you have time to compose yourself once there.

Be respectful, courteous, and truthful. While this goes almost without saying, some interviewers intentionally will try to rile you up to see how you will react. Others simply have no idea how to interview. Keep your emotions and defensiveness in check, no matter how well-justified they may seem to you. Remain composed at all times and always answer questions honestly.

Be a good listener. As much as you want to tell all, resist the temptation. Listen to what the interviewer says and asks, then respond appropriately. Check in with the interviewer and ask, "Does that answer your question?" Do this often, because it is only through feedback that you will know if you have responded too little, too much, or just right.

Assess your poker hand objectively. Most of us enter interviews with a certain emotional trepidation. Obviously, a lot is at stake. But it is important to assess how valuable your skills are to the employer. Note the signals sent out to you already. Don't be overly optimistic or overly pessimistic. Before the interview, exchange ideas with a trusted confidant. Try to ascertain your relative position in the prospective company's eyes. There are often signs that you might be the favored candidate or only candidate. Therefore, the job might be yours for the taking as long as you remain calm and reasonable. On the other hand, you might talk yourself out of a job (literally).

Interview the company. The interview should be a two-way street. Not only does the company want to learn if you will meet its needs, but also you want to figure out if the company meets your needs. Therefore, ask questions about the company on major issues of concern to you, such as:

How does the company allow people to use their own initiative?

How are people recognized for achievement?

How are people allowed to have a say in decisions from above that would impact their own jobs?

Is there autonomy on how the job gets done once an agreement is reached on what is to be done?

Are there regular feedback mechanisms in place?

Is there an ongoing program or policy regarding training for newly needed skills?

Rehearse the awkward questions you can expect. Regardless of roles and industries, many interview questions are predictable. Imagine these typical interview stumpers:

What are your strengths?

What are your weaknesses?

Why should I hire you?

What can you bring to this job?

Here are some examples of how you can use your PAVF work style as a starting point for these awkward questions during an interview:

What are your strengths? "I drive for results (P) and find creative new solutions to problems (V)."

What are your weaknesses? "I like to get things done, and can appear pushy or impatient as a result (P)." Or, "I prefer variety and novelty because I like to innovate, rather than repeat." (V)

Why should I hire you? "You should hire me because I am driven to get things done (P) and thrive on innovation, creativity, and practical solutions (V)."

What can you bring to this job? "I will get things done in a timely manner (P) and enjoy discovering new approaches to challenges that arise (V)."

Because you used the PAVF Work-Styles Profiling Survey as the starting point for all your reflection and packaging work to date (Sections 1 and 2), you can easily address these questions truthfully and confidently by reiterating the appropriate aspects of your story (Section 2).

Preparing for other types of evaluations, assessment centers, and psychometrics. There is really no way to prepare for these, but we have a very strong recommendation: be yourself. If you try to second-guess the psychometric answers, that will be detected. Many of them have a score which reflects how much you have (or have not) tried to engineer a result. Assessment centers can be grueling (which is why they are a much better way of evaluating candidates), so get a good night's sleep, and (again) be yourself.

Keep control of the situation. Of course, you do not control the interview, but you can control your answers. Also, avoid playing the waiting game. Identify every next step of the process by asking the interviewer what it is: "When do you expect to be making a decision by?" If the interviewer or company representative does not establish next steps, take a proactive stance and try to set expectations.

Stage 4: Negotiating and Closing

At this point, your networking focus and persistence has generated positive outcomes. You have interviewed for a specific position (or contract opportunity) and are now engaging in negotiations to formally close the position. In our experience, many people have difficulty navigating themselves into a position of relative strength to negotiate from. We provide very detailed recommendations on how to do this effectively. Strong negotiating on your part may improve your overall compensation package by 10% to 25% annually, so it is well worth it to really absorb the next several pages.

Step 1: Negotiating your package

For most people, negotiating salary is difficult. Try to think of it from another perspective: you're discovering what money the company has allocated for someone with your skills in this role. When you have accepted a position and salary discussions begin, the employer will have a salary figure upfront based on market expectations and comparable salaries within the company. The employer knows this number, but you don't; your challenge is to determine how much the company is willing to pay for the position.

The employer (or HR) expects you to negotiate. You want to collect as much as possible. It would be a shame to leave money on the table. If companies are willing to pay more for a position, and you are qualified, you should be compensated accordingly. In preparing for your negotiations, keep the following in mind:

Research salaries in your field;

Negotiate your salary from a position of strength;

Let them make the first offer;

Silence is golden—and your most powerful negotiating tool;

Respond to offers;

Negotiate benefits once the salary is finalized;

Work with two or more firm offers;

Get your offer in writing.

Let's review each point in depth.

Research salaries in your field. By researching the salary beforehand, you will know if you are getting a fair deal. The better prepared you are, the better armed you are for the salary talks. Salaryexpert.com is an excellent resource that allows you to customize your search around location, competencies, and years of experience. You might also look to appropriate professional association and trade journals and your network (recruiters, peers, network associates) for further data points. For the truly proactive person, here is an interesting do-it-yourself method: Say you're interviewing for a position as a customer service representative. Choose six companies with similar positions. Call each one if you can, and ask to talk to their customer service representative. Explain to the representative you're negotiating salary for a similar position and name the responsibilities. Ask what the pay range for this position is in his or her organization; tell the representative you are calling a number of others and that you'll compile and share the results with all. They'll participate because they're just as curious as you about their own worth in the open market. Get their contact information so you can keep your promise and send the results.

Negotiate your salary from a position of strength. If you engage in salary discussions before you are offered a job, you will have almost no bargaining position. You want to negotiate from a position of strength, so wait until the job offer. Once you know they want you, you are in a much stronger position. An interesting role reversal takes place if you postpone salary discussions until offer time. Interviews start with employers buying and you selling. If you postpone discussing salary, however, the role is reversed. They are in a position where they want you. They've decided to ask you to join them, so they're selling the job to you. This is the only time they'll be anxious to reel you in. Further, HR or the negotiators do not want to lose face. Here are some approaches to build into your strategy:

Respond confidently to any premature salary gambits on their part:

"I'm sure we can come to a fair salary agreement if I'm the right person for the job, so let's agree on that first."

"Salary? Well, so far, the job seems to have the right amount of responsibility for me and I'm sure you pay a fair salary, don't you?"

Soften your approach with honesty:

"Discussing salary is always awkward for me, so..."

"When we discuss money upfront, I get worried I'll be screened out or boxed in, so could we...?"

Ask questions to find out what's so important about knowing your salary requirements:

"I notice we're back on salary again. May I ask you a question? Are you wondering if you can afford me? Or do you just need it for an application? Or is there something else?"

"I notice we've come back to salary. I'm happy to discuss money, and even share my tax return with you at some point if it's important. But is it possible to take a moment to explain why we need to discuss it now?"

Close with a strong wrap-up:

"I'm sure we can come to a fair salary agreement when the time comes."

"I know I need to make you more than I cost. Let's make sure the fit is right before we discuss salary."

"Maybe you've noticed by now that it's a principle of mine never to discuss salary upfront. If we're going to work together, we'll have to respect each other's principles, so let's focus on how I can help you make money."

"Most people I talk to say salary is just the finishing touch to the person who can play for the team. Let's talk about money as soon as we're sure I'm the player you're after."

"I don't want to appear difficult. I can understand that you want to be sure you can afford me, and I won't require a salary out of line with the job. But it's a principle of mine not to discuss salary yet, because it can throw us off track. What's really important is whether I'm right for the job and what I can produce for you."

"Compensation is about third on my priorities list right now. First is making sure we can work together, and I'd prefer to concentrate on that for now."

If they insist you have to commit first, ask questions to find out what they have in mind:

"Well, I'm sure you have something budgeted for this position. What range did you have in mind?"

"I have some idea of the market, but I'd be interested in starting with your range for the moment."

When asked about present or previous salary:

"I'm paid very fairly for my responsibilities in my present job, and I expect a fair salary with respect to my responsibilities here."

Regardless if an ad demands your salary history or expectations, employers will not pass you over if you're right for the job, provided you show them respect. Employers want these figures as part of their screening process. They don't want to waste time talking to you if they can't afford you. Your best approach is to acknowledge the need to screen, then stick to your principles about postponing money talks until there's a match. In your cover letter, write something such as:

"You've requested a salary history. I'm paid roughly the market value of a [Job Title] with X years' experience, and though I'm not willing to publish my compensation package, I'd be happy to discuss it in an interview. I am sure salary will not be a problem for me for this position."

When an application form asks for salary expectations, write "Open." When it asks for previous salary history, leave it blank.

If the application states, "Fill in every blank and answer every question," put "competitive" in the salary slot and write a note at the bottom: "I'll be glad to discuss this personally in an interview."

If you are filling out an application form online that lists salary as a required field, attempt to put in a range. If it does not allow a range, only a specific number, it is even more difficult. In either case, follow the processes below:

After having done your research, decide on a minimum acceptable salary to you, and then add $5,000 to that number. That will be the bottom of your range. For example: If you would accept $45,000 for a job, your bottom range will be $50,000 ($45,000+$5,000). Then, decide on a salary that would make you feel fairly compensated for this job, and add another $10,000. This will be the top of your range. For example, if you think you are worth $65,000, then the top of your range will be $75,000. Thus, your range will be $50,000–$75,000. Ranges should span at least $20,000.

If the application form allows only a specified number, put in the higher figure (namely $75,000). However, in your salary negotiation strategy, be prepared to bump this figure up further because they are preparing to bump it down.

Managing your response to the salary question takes practice. If getting them to make the first offer adds thousands of extra dollars into your pocket, it will be well worth the extra discipline required on your part.

Silence can be golden... literally: Your most valuable negotiation tool is to say nothing. Not only is it the most effective approach, but it also does not compromise your principles of being respectful of others, and keeps you modest and non-confrontational.

At this point, you've done your salary research, deferred any salary discussion and negotiation until an offer has been extended, and extracted a salary number from the employer. Here is what you need to do now:

When you hear that figure or range, repeat the number in a contemplative tone. Count to thirty silently. This will feel like an eternity, but stay silent; those 30 seconds can yield you extra money.

Use this time to calculate exactly what the offer is. For example, you can convert an hourly figure to a yearly figure by doubling it in thousands. So $18 an hour is about $36,000, based on forty hours a week with no overtime. To go from weekly to yearly, multiply by 50; for example, $1,000 a week equals $50,000 a year.

With the stage now set, you want to pursue the following goals simultaneously:

Let them counteroffer: For most interviewers, that silence will be devastating and uncomfortable. In 99% of the cases, they will break the silence: "Is something wrong?", "Is it not enough?", or, "We can up the offer by $4,000, but not a cent more." Respond to the first two questions with, "I was hoping for a bit more." If there is a counteroffer, repeat the figure aloud and again go into silence mode.

Find out what is in their "bank vault": During this silence, they may come back with another offer, or ask: "Exactly what were you expecting?" Reply with a figure well above their offer. You do not need to justify or rationalize it—this is not about fairness, but merely the value they have placed on the job. "I was hoping in the high sixties." Two possibilities now exist. First, if your statement is still within their means and they feel you are worth it, they will move closer to this number. They might suggest: "We might be able to reach a little deeper, but it's not easy for us." Asking, "How deep?" will prompt them to offer a new figure, which you should contemplate in silence... again. The second possibility is they can't meet your desired range: "I'm afraid we just can't go any higher for this position," or, "We really want you as part of our team, but we have to get permission from higher authority." You have achieved your goal of assessing the contents of the bank vault, so be careful here: the higher authority could reject your offer, and you don't want to come across as unreasonable.

Responding with the truth: Be honest: "Sounds great," "Sounds acceptable," or, "Sounds disappointing." You'll know if the range is fair because you researched your market value beforehand. *Don't compare the offer with your most recent salary.* Instead, use those thirty seconds to compare the offer with your research. Grounded in your knowledge of the market value for the position and your experience, you'll have calculated two figures before going into the interview—the highest you're worth and the lowest you'll accept. On the other hand, all the research in the world won't help if the company has a different idea about the salaries it pays.

Step 2: Responding to a first offer

While an offer on the table that is too high seems like a pleasant problem to have, it does deserve some attention. If your employer makes the mistake of overpaying you, the company will regret the deal and resent you in the long run. Sometimes you will encounter employers so anxious to have you that they load up their offer with the best deal they can make. You'll recognize it because it will catch you by surprise. On the other hand, when the offer is too low, don't give up! First, acknowledge the offer positively: "Thirty-five thousand dollars... I appreciate your offer, and I'd love to work here. I'm sure you want to pay me a fair compensation that will keep me committed and productive. From my research, I estimate that positions like this for someone with my qualifications are paying in the range of X to Y thousand dollars. What can you do in that range?" The range you give will bracket the high end of your research. For example, if your research uncovered a range of $35,000 to $38,000, counteroffer with $37,000 to $40,000. Typically, your interviewer will let you know what the company can do in that range. Never say, "Well, I couldn't possibly go below $35,000." Employers will presume that figure to be padded and may counter with something lower. Ask for the top range if you believe you merit it. Otherwise, settle for a middle range. Even if you're entry level, add $1,000 to $2,000 to your minimum range. The worst they can do is say no. Many people think they'll lose an employer's respect if they talk extensively about money. That's true before the offer, but after an offer, it can actually increase respect.

If you can't reach a mutually satisfying salary, you still have the lower offer. Don't say no right away. Let the employer sweat a little. Remember, the company wants you. Tell the employer you're still very excited about the opportunity and you want to think about it and talk again. In addition, consider the rest of the compensation package besides base salary. Negotiating profit sharing, benefits, bonuses, stock options, vacation time, accelerated commission scales, an entertainment budget, or a company car is another way to build your overall compensation package. In the case when you are not at the salary level you want, aim for additional compensation in other areas, such as an extra week's vacation. In fact, we strongly recommend that you use this strategy whether or not they meet your number. After they have explained they can't go any higher in salary, offer up: "You know, we can have a deal if you toss in two more weeks of vacation." Then let the dialog of silence-and-offer continue.

Finally, don't say "yes" right away either! Financial decisions are best made in the cool climate of logic and impartiality. Give yourself time to think, but don't appear indifferent or undecided. When you've finished negotiating, always start with the good news: "This sounds terrific! I think we've really got a solid match here! Would you write all this down so we're clear? I'll get back to you as soon as possible.

When do you need my answer?" Maintain your enthusiasm so your request for extra time isn't misconstrued as a lack of interest. There's a delicate line here between demanding time and requesting clarity. How do you ask for more time? Here are some ideas:

> "Thank you! This is a great opportunity. I'll need to look this over to make sure we haven't forgotten anything, so when do you need my final answer?"
>
> "Okay, I'm giving a tentative 'yes' for now and I'll give you my final answer as soon as you need it. When would that be?"
>
> "I will sleep on this, look at it again to make sure we covered everything, and confirm it in writing by [date]."

Step 3: Negotiating your benefits package

Once the salary is finalized, you can focus on the benefits. Your first priority is your take-home pay, followed by commissions and bonuses. Your next priority is the benefits. Things to consider in the benefits discussion:

> **Salary reviews.** The first thing to explore is the salary review. One of the reasons for negotiating the best base salary first is that raises are generally computed as a percentage of that base. There are three areas to consider in a review negotiation: percentage, timing, and basis for increases. Although you can't predict the actual percentage of a future raise now, you can influence it by taking a look at any Cost-of-Living Adjustment (COLA) —an automatic raise to compensate for inflation. You can bring up the subject of a salary review by talking first about COLA and the company's policy. Make sure you understand the salary review process and how it works.
>
> **Sales compensation.** If you are in sales, you typically earn commissions. You can try to negotiate higher commission rates. If those are standardized and nonnegotiable, try asking for a higher

commission rate over a certain quota. For example, if normal sales are $40,000 to $50,000 a month, with a 5% commission, you can ask that sales over $50,000 a month receive a 6% commission.

Performance bonuses. Bonuses are based on your performance, and give you an incentive to work harder and make your employer more money. You can negotiate your own version of that, no matter what your job. You must pin a mutually agreeable number to the quantity or quality of your work using objectively measurable criteria. Pose an open-ended question to the employer: "I'd like to consider setting up a special bonus to encourage excellent performance. Do you have ideas or experiences with a workable one?" **Stock options** traditionally have been offered only to executives and the highest levels of corporate management. Nowadays, they are available to lower levels of management or all employees. Some of the most successful companies have what are known as Employee Stock Ownership Programs (ESOP). **Profit sharing** is rarely discussed in a job interview, but you can suggest it if you know your work has a direct impact on company profits. Profit sharing is usually computed quarterly or annually.

Other benefits. Most people find negotiating for additional benefits stressful. If you fall into this category, then stop when you get the pay you want. You are 85% to 95% of where you want to be. On the other hand, if the salary isn't quite what you expected, adding some nontaxable extras can bring the entire offer very close to the figure you had in mind. Consider the following opportunities:

> **Relocation expenses.** Relocation expenses aren't always offered. With a new employer, paying for relocation is common only in executive positions, or when the employer wants you badly enough. Some relocation perks include company purchase of your present or future home; company payment of moving fees, closing costs, real estate broker fees, any mortgage cancellation penalty, mortgage rate differentials, transportation costs to look at new homes, appliance installation, and lodging fees while looking or waiting for a new home.

Vacation and personal days. Negotiate vacation, personal days, or your hours per week. First, ask about the company's vacation and time off policies. See if you can negotiate another week of vacation or a few extra personal days.

Transportation. For positions involving a lot of travel, discuss travel and mileage allowances or the possibility of a company car or car allowance. A company car will help you save money on insurance, maintenance, and depreciation costs on your own vehicle, and may save you much of the tax on those expenses.

Home office. See if your employer is willing to pay some of your home office expenses that can offset your usual out-of-pocket costs. Working from home at least a day or two a week is becoming more of a standard in many industries.

Expense accounts. Another benefit to address now is expense accounts or entertainment accounts, especially if you are in sales. What does the company consider customary expenses, and are there exceptions?

Insurance and health benefits. Inquire about the company's health benefits and insurance plan—they vary greatly from company to company, so ask to see the plan and coverage. If you are unemployed and currently paying your own insurance, you may negotiate instant insurance coverage rather than after the typical three-month waiting period.

Professional memberships. If a professional membership will increase your productivity, the employer should be willing to pay your membership dues and give you time off for meetings or events.

Tuition reimbursement. Are there specific courses or degrees that would help you perform your job better? Ask about the company's continuing education policy.

Step 4: Working to create multiple offers

Since your negotiating power jumps dramatically if you can work one offer against another, your attempt to work toward two job offers makes sense. You might be nervous about waiting for a second offer, take the first job offered, and be happy with your decision. However, we have seen salaries jump substantially once the employer learned there might be another bid on the table. Not only that, we have seen situations where the second offer, while not the original preferred choice, becomes the prominent offer.

Creating the second offer. Once the first offer comes forward, it behooves you to find a second one; it is probably not as far off as you think. There may be other job opportunities through your ongoing Exploration Meetings and networking activities. Reach out to your contacts and tell them about your offer: “Ms. Jones, we spoke two weeks ago about some possible job openings in the mineralogy group. I know there was nothing definite, but I’m calling you because of a change in my situation. I have just been offered a job with Alpha Minerals, which I am tempted to take, but frankly, I found your group very appealing. If any opportunities have come along, could you let me know as soon as possible?” Even if the company does not have an opportunity or interest, it will make no difference to you, and only cost you a few minutes. If the company does have a position available and is receptive, reveal that you are interested, but only have a brief window in which to act. The company will need to respond now or lose you. If you approach five or so companies, one will probably respond and ask if you are available for an interview or how much time they have to make a decision. Do not feel bad about drawing less-important job prospects into the mix. As we said earlier, we have seen these ‘less-important’ prospects turn into the winning opportunity. You never know what is going to happen.

Let’s assume you receive a second job offer. Company A wants a decision that day and Company B’s offer will take five days to be formalized. Suggest your own time frame and see if Company A can work within it: "This job meets all my criteria, and I truly feel this is a good match, but I want to consider it very carefully. I'd like one week to think it over. Will that work with your schedule?" Sometimes it will, sometimes it won't. Often, you're comparing a bird in the hand with two in the bush. When buying time, don’t concentrate on the first offer, but focus on accelerating the second offer. If your second offer has any merit, that means you have established a good relationship with the hiring individual. Use that rapport. Have a face-to-face meeting with the manager of Company B, explain the situation, and ask for assistance: "I have another offer in front of me (A). The jobs are fairly different. Frankly, my preference is to take the one in which I can make the best contribution. How can we get things moving here to meet the short deadline of the first offer?" If you have good rapport with the manager, you can work together to accelerate things. If the manager will not work with you, that's a strong indication the company might be a poor fit. Assuming multiple offers, examine the offers and give each of them grades in areas of importance to you (for example: satisfaction, professional growth, responsibility, location, people, company style, and compensation). Write down your priorities on a chart and then number each one in order of importance; reorganize them with your highest priority first, and compare the jobs point by point.

Step 5: Finalizing and accepting an offer

Get the offer(s) in writing. Having the employer recap the offer in writing is crucial in these expedient situations. Things are moving fast, and you want to know your negotiations will not get lost in the shuffle—and if it's not written down, something will get lost in the shuffle.

In a normal-paced situation, as long as you have agreed to a definite acceptance date, there should be no danger of losing an offer. While you probably can wait for a formal offer letter from the employer, we recommend you **get confirmation of the offer in writing** (even if just a brief note). Written documentation avoids anyone reneging, and it also reassures you are both on the same page.

> **Document detailed situations carefully,** such as those involving special provisions, fees, or expenses. If the offer is more complicated than the standard one of salary, benefits, and starting date, get it in writing immediately. It doesn't have to be to be a formal letter on letterhead—write the details down neatly during the interview, date it, and ask your employer to look it over. Be sure to make a copy for your personal records.
>
> **Leaving one job for another.** If you have to resign from a current position, definitely get an official formal letter in writing first. Do not give notice at your current job until you have a formal letter.
>
> **Ensuring immediate confirmation.** Sometimes it can take companies up to several weeks to send you a formal offer letter or job contract. Therefore, insist on a brief summary of the job highlights within a day or two from the person for whom you will directly work. Minimize its importance and emphasize it doesn't need to be long or overly detailed. However, make sure the letter contains the actual offer, start date, job title, your manager, and main salary, with a mention of other compensation.

Avoid formality. If you discover some discrepancy in the summary, resolve it quickly. Be less formal and notate the changes on the letter, getting both parties to initial the changes.

Telephone acceptance. An offer acceptance can be done by phone. Take the time you need to think about the offer and then call to accept. When you call the company, request both a confirmation letter and a more formal written offer. In well-managed companies, the Personnel or Human Resources departments will provide the formal offer within a week. However, most companies are not so well managed, hence the need for the confirmation letter.

Wrap-up. Communicate your enthusiasm once again for the job and the company, and assure your employer how well you expect this to work out.

Step 6: Celebrating (and writing about it)!

No matter how you landed that unbelievable dream job, contract, or growth opportunity—whether through a pro-bono gig, an Exploration Meeting, or volunteering your time and expertise—you should celebrate your success with loved ones and your supporters. Express how much you truly appreciate their help and support. Reflect on this win in your journal; how it came about, how you are feeling about it, and the road you traveled to get there. Continued journaling about your experiences, the steps and feedback you've received along the way, and the ultimate outcome will all add to your continued discipline and motivation to continue down this new path.

SECTION THREE: Recap

This section covered the elements required to enhance your ongoing networking activities as you explore interesting, appealing opportunities.

> We took you through a detailed explanation of how most people think the job market works versus the actual reality of human engagement, **the "real hiring process."** We discussed the **hidden job market** and mentioned the roles of employment agencies and recruiters. You learned how to structure your own job search. We advocated for you to reverse your efforts from firing out résumés to **disciplined networking.**
>
> To help improve your networking effectiveness, we discussed some of the basic scientific principles of human connections, network creation, and propagation. We touched on how to get the most out of **group networking events** and how to **set up and manage successful Exploration Meetings** (these are the backbone of your networking efforts).
>
> We gave instructions on how to build and **manage your own opportunity pipeline.** You also worked through several specific ideas about **what kinds of opportunities were relevant** to you, and learned how to construct **useful criteria for deciding which opportunities to pursue.**
>
> We then discussed how you convert opportunities to actual deals. We focused extensively on converting job opportunities into formal job offers; we covered how to **compile cover letters, have a successful formal interview,** and **negotiate from a position of strength.** We placed great emphasis on these because they are a big challenge for most job seekers, and lack of thorough preparation carries the greatest cost.

You now have much greater clarity about what you are looking for, a compelling story to tell people about how you add value, and you are on the path to becoming a much more effective networker. Importantly, your active job search time hasn't increased; you're just using the same amount of time more effectively. The payoff for all this hard work is an opportunity pipeline brimming with interesting conversations, uncovering new information sources, and discovering great-fit opportunities. Keep working your pipeline and before you know it, you'll have landed that perfect job!

CONCLUSION

We would like to thank and acknowledge you for dedicating yourself to this career (re)boot. If you found this process valuable, please stay connected with us through our websites – we intend to offer webinars, audio books, blogs, workshops and other "reboot" tools over the coming year. There may shortly be other books in the "Reboot" series, and Tim's company, Career Constructors, has a suite of powerful offerings should you wish more extensive support in your career journey. Paul is an author of books with science at their core but with practical implications for people and business leaders – he releases a new book every 18-24 months.

Tim's website is http://careerconstructors.com

Paul's is http://www.paulgibbons.net

In the section that follows, we recap some of the key ideas. Learning theory teaches that such a review greatly improves retention. Following that, we offer a few final paragraphs with some critical tips.

Recap of Your "Reboot" Process

Upon completing the full set of exercises you will feel more confident about yourself and your inner strengths (Section 1), what you have to offer the world in terms of how you best add value (Section 2), and how to effectively take that message out into the world and help create your best fit opportunities (Section 3).

As you review what you have done, reflect on any of the sections, stages, or steps that you are having trouble completing, or that you feel didn't really gel for you when you first worked through them. Now that you've gone through the complete process, do those make more sense? Make a note of any that you would like to come back to at some stage, and plan a time to go back and refresh your work.

INTRODUCTION: Careers in the 21st Century

The thrust of our introduction was that careers and work in the 21st century are radically different from a few decades ago. Whether referred to as precarious work, the gig economy, freelancing, contracting, or any other term, success demands remaining agile, anticipating change, and continually seeking out new opportunities, and evolving your value proposition. Andy Grove (long serving CEO of Intel) famously suggested that "only the paranoid survive". It's good advice for today's careers– be "paranoid" that your current role will be outsourced, automated, made redundant, or otherwise made to disappear. That is the nature of organizations. You will be more attuned to the changing big picture in your firm, industry, or sector and better placed to do something proactive about it.

SECTION ONE: The "Inside Job" - Building Your Foundation

Flourishing. It is too easy to just say "I'm not happy" and then get stressed out thinking about what you should do about it. We introduced the **flourishing** exercises to get you to drill a little deeper into what specifically you aren't happy about. This basic diagnostic tool allows you to quickly get a better handle on what aspect of your career (or life) isn't working for you. As with many things in our careers, the more specificity you can muster at this first stage the more you are able to take meaningful action(s) rather than flailing about and jumping from the fry pan into the fire. Ouch!

PAVF workstyles. With the **PAVF Work Styles profile**, you started the real journey of figuring out your internal wiring. The output to this piece of our process is finding the key words (descriptors) around which you want to build your story. They have to feel authentic and feel powerful to you, so you can deliver them with passion in your career-related communication. These are the words that ultimately help describe how you live and breathe every day of your life.

Showcasing accomplishments. No matter who you are, you've done a bunch of cool things in your life, and because you've done them so naturally, you don't think they are anything special. It is human nature to downplay our own accomplishments because we've been socialized from an early age that "bragging isn't nice". The people around us see us differently – they see our natural abilities much more clearly than we do, and when they comment on them ("Wow, you're great at that!), we deflect and put ourselves down ("That? It was nothing. Anybody could do that."). Wrong – your buddy is telling you that not anybody can do it, but you can. The **accomplishments** section was about identifying and owning what you have accomplished, and starting to feel confident about showcasing it. It takes time and effort because we have to overcome our "gee shucks" socialization. Remember, it's not bragging if it is true and quantifiable. It's impressive. Own it.

Mission, vision, values. It's so easy in our society to get "off track" if we don't have a clear touchstone about what's important to us – that is what mission, vision and values is all about. These are the components that crystallize our purpose. While it is challenging work to discover our true purpose, it is actually pretty easy to tell when we are off kilter and working against our purpose. That is that voice deep in your gut that says "Whoa, wait a minute. This isn't me!" It's that negative stress you feel about your work, your environment, your life. Your body is sending you these signals all the time. Listen to them, embrace them, and do the reflective work to help you discover your purpose. You'll put it to good use every time you need to reach a decision about what opportunities to pursue, and what actions to take.

SECTION TWO: Developing a Personal Brand – Your Compelling Value Story

This section was about taking the great internal work ("the inside job") from Section 1, and crafting your personal brand ("compelling value story").

Résumés. When people embark upon a career transition, they often jump directly to updating their résumé and then pumping it out into the vastness of the internet. Most résumés are dull because people look backward and try to say far too much: ("Look at all the important titles and roles I've had. There is so much to share with you I need several pages, because all the nitty-gritty detail is super important. I'm sure you can find a way to use me. Please call!"). A great résumé starts with a tight future-oriented statement ("Here is what I can do for you, and why you can believe I'll perform brilliantly.") Don't dash off your résumé and make stuff up on the fly; take your time to really construct a suitable container for your powerful story.

LinkedIn. LinkedIn is by far the most important social media tool for professionals. Thirty or forty people a week may look at your profile (depending on how much you do). We gave you a structure for a kickbutt profile, and guidance for contributing to LinkedIn discussions and getting a lot more from your time invested in LinkedIn.

Social media. You want to use social media and not have it use you – that is, make conscious decisions about what, when, how often, and how you respond. That means turning it off when you have to work, turning off all notifications on all devices, and being disciplined. Used correctly, you can reinforce your personal brand, but to get the most bang for your buck, you want to build and engage a community of people that are interested in what you have to offer (your personal brand), and that you add value to (your insights, contacts, content), and that in turn can add value to you (their insights, contacts, content). It all stems from having a clear social media strategy.

SECTION THREE: The "Outside Job" – Modern Networking and Job Hunting

Networking. The problem is that most people hate networking, aren't really good at it, and so shy away from it and put the bulk of their job search time into applying for posted roles. This is a waste of time: the job market works very differently from how you probably think it does -- – understanding this makes you more willing to use your time differently. We also spent some time laying out the fundamentals of how humans connect, so that you can build this knowledge into your own networking activities. And to really make the point that effective networking requires taking action, we implored you to start setting up meetings and scheduling events to network at. Have you done that yet?

Network events. This is really the "how-to" piece of the networking puzzle. The whole point of putting yourself out there (events, Exploration Meetings, social media activities) is to collide with humanity, share your story, and generate potential opportunities where you can do stuff that matters to you. Of course opportunities come in various different shapes and sizes and a lot of them require a lot of work to knock them into something that really fits. Thomas Edison is reputed to have said: "Opportunity is missed because it is dressed in overalls and looks like work." You have to get off your backside, get out there (virtually and in the real world) and engage with people to make opportunities happen.

We showed you how and provided the basic tools. Keep working this, keep persisting, and good things will start to happen.

Job-hunting. While opportunities come in all shapes and sizes, the formal job application and related process is pretty standard across the working world. And when you are dealing with the formal work world, they are pretty sticky about you following their defined process, dotting all your i's and crossing all your t's. So play their game and follow their specified process. Luckily most of them aren't very imaginative so the generic steps we provide for how to complete your application, write your cover letter, submit your résumé and prepare for your interviews will be applicable to all of your formal applications.

Negotiating. Somebody is really interested in you and has made an initial offer. Wait! Don't accept it blindly – you're better than that, because you've now spent a lot of time crafting your story and getting to the heart of your real value. It is at this point where some savvy negotiating skills on your part will probably improve your overall package by a decent amount, perhaps as much as 25%. So we shared a bunch of tips and strategies for how to do just that, including canvassing the landscape for a competing offer to create a bit of competition for the employer to deal with. Remain humble, and clear about how valuable you are in the right setting. Keep working what we've laid out for you and you'll be accepting that brilliant offer in short order.

Final Thoughts

Having worked diligently through the exercises, you have a solid foundation for your career. There will inevitably be more to do. We gave you a recipe that will allow you to design and re-design your career in the future.

Most of us need support – get some!

Having worked through this material many, many times with various clients, we realize that people can struggle with some of the stages and exercises. Those people really benefit from support throughout the process while a few others are self-directed and jump in happily with both feet. If you have struggled with some of the stages and steps, don't lose confidence – getting this stuff to gel is tough going for many people and takes time, deep reflection, and generous amounts of encouragement and involvement from trusted confidants and coaches.

At many points in our process we recommended that you engage trusted confidants. If you don't feel that you have people you trust enough to share this journey with, then consider investing in a career coach. A good career coach, one who is a good fit for you, is an excellent way to accelerate your way through this process.

First follow the recipe, then innovate

The first time you use our tools, you should "stick fairly close to the recipe", as you would in cooking something for the first time. Once comfortable, you can innovate – spice things up, try different combinations.

Rinse and repeat

Your story evolves as you discover new opportunities, add new skills to your mix, take on new assignments and learn new things about yourself.

Keep this book handy and revisit the exercises on a regular basis. Play around with new words (descriptors) as you come across words and phrases that are emotionally impactful to you. Keep reviewing and honing your accomplishments, and add your new accomplishments into your inventory. Review your mission, vision and values and continue to tighten the concepts and your language as you continue to solidify your "true purpose". Play around with the opportunity pipeline concepts and develop your own system that really works for you.

Celebrate!

Please, please, please don't ignore the final step in our process – take those you love and those that are supporting you in your journey out and celebrate your "wins" along the way. Life is, after all, a team sport and this is your team. Let them know how important they are to your continuing success. Congratulations on your continuing dedication and persistence in successfully (re)booting your career!

ABOUT THE AUTHORS

Tim Ragan is a strategy consultant, business operator, team facilitator, researcher, and author. He is fascinated with high performance and the process of transformation, and has discovered (through much experimentation) that he is most alive when working directly with individuals, work teams, and organizations to measurably improve their performance and mission effectiveness. He has university degrees in electrical engineering and business administration and lives in Ottawa, Canada, with his partner Colleen.

Paul Gibbons is an author, speaker, and consultant. His "beat" is helping business leaders use science and philosophy to make better strategic decisions, implement change, innovate, change culture, and create workplaces where talent flourishes. His most recent book, The Science of Organizational Change has been hailed as "the most important book on change in fifteen years." Between writing projects, he consults, coaches, and speaks with businesses such as Microsoft, Google, HSBC, KPMG, and Comcast

Acknowledgements

We want to acknowledge the support, guidance, and intellectual property that Bill Caswell gave to this project. Bill founded Career Coaching International (CCI) which Tim subsequently purchased and rebranded to Career Constructors (http://careerconstructors.com). Bill and CCI's client-centric approach formed the original skeleton of our career reboot process; ownership of the PAVF methodology and associated tools remains with Bill Caswell. Additionally, Bill has reviewed various drafts of this book and provided invaluable input.

We also wish to acknowledge the support of many people who have provided feedback on our manuscript and have taken the time to review drafts and provide suggestions for improvement. In no particular order, we wish to thank Brooklyn Currie, Len Fardella, Andy Church, Britt-Mari Sykes, and Greg O'Donnell for their efforts reviewing drafts and providing constructive input. David Sigler provided early draft material on some sections, notably the detailed social media material.

Finally, we would like to thank our editorial and production team including Anita Chiquita (proofreading), Alex Irwin (formatting), and Andrés Goldstein (cover and illustrations).

Made in the USA
San Bernardino, CA
27 April 2018